D0537759

Cry Myself to Sleep

Cry Myself to Sleep

He had to escape. They would never hurt him again.

JOE PETERS

with Andrew Crofts

HarperElement
An Imprint of HarperCollins*Publishers*
77–85 Fulham Palace Road,
Hammersmith, London W6 8JB

www.harpercollins.co.uk

and *HarperElement* are trademarks
of HarperCollins*Publishers* Ltd

First published by HarperElement 2009

10 9 8 7 6 5 4 3 2 1

A catalogue record of this book is
available from the British Library

ISBN 978-0-00-727504-5

Printed and bound in Great Britain by
Clays Ltd, St Ives plc

In loving memory of my wonderful dad 'George William', 1944–78.

Thanks for those early years together. These memories I will treasure for a lifetime; until the day we meet again I accept you're here by my side in spirit.

To my baby that I never got to see, may God rest your soul. Granddad will look after you until the day we meet in heaven and I finally get to see you.

In my thoughts all the time.

Love,

Dad x

Acknowledgements

Dear young brother,
You have come far and grown to understand so
much, and life has been tough for you. I know things
are bad for you at the moment, but my strength and
love will carry us both in these hard times.
Loving you always,
Your big brother x

To my five heroes: Darren, Liam, Kirsty-Lea, Shannon
and Paige.
You make me laugh, you make me cry and the years
have gone nowhere! You are growing into strong-
minded individuals and I am so proud of you all; I am
proud to be your Dad.
Whatever path you choose in life I will always be
here for you.
Love, Dad x

To Michelle,
The woman and soulmate who has taught me a lot
in life, who lights up my darkest moments and keeps
me on track!
I hope we have many more years of great love
together x

To Sue (my adopted mum in Penzance) and my
extended family there, Tammy, Kirsti, Lee and Sam.
Love you all always xxx

To Andy Reeve and Partner,
St Leonards Equitation Centre,
Launceston,
Thanks, Andy, for taking me on, and giving me the
chance that nobody else would.

To Police Constable Christopher Thomas and
Pontycymmer police station,
For your community support and wonderful
understanding with me and my family.

To our best and loyal friends, Mike Morgan and Sarah
Finch.
Love you both to bits – keep on writing Mike.
X

And finally to all my great readers and supporters, You are all my close friends, thank you so much for being there for me, sticking by me and supporting me throughout my campaign and my ill health. You all mean so much to me and my work.

Cry Myself
to Sleep

Chapter One

My Life Goes up in Flames

I was only five years old and my father was the centre of my universe. I knew he was the most important person in my short life, but what I couldn't possibly know at that terrible moment was that he had been the only protection I had from enemies I didn't even realize I possessed. I knew that I loved him far more than I loved Mum and I knew that he loved me with the same intensity, that I was 'his boy'; but I didn't realize how much Mum hated me for being Dad's favourite, or how much my half brothers wanted to hurt me.

Mum and Dad's marriage was in tatters by that time, and Mum must have seen me as being on his side and so loathed me in the same way that she loathed him. I knew she was capable of physically hurting me, because she had done so in the past, but I had no idea how far she would be prepared to go in the coming years.

1

On the day when everything changed for ever I watched my father burning to death in front of my eyes. I could do nothing to help him as he ran around the garage in flames, screaming from the pain while I struggled to escape from the car, where he had left me in order to go to work. It was as if everything was happening in slow motion and all the other grown-ups were rooted to the spot by the horror of what they were witnessing. There had been a smell of petrol and a carelessly thrown cigarette end which had been caught by the wind and blown back into the building, igniting the spilled fuel and turning my father into a living torch as he worked underneath the engine. Eventually I fought free of the car and ran to help him, but someone grabbed me and held me tight before I could reach him.

Dad never recovered consciousness after the ambulance took him away, and Mum instructed the doctors to turn off his life-support machine a few days later. I had to listen while she and Marie, Dad's girlfriend, fought about it in the hospital, and then fought about me. Even though I wanted to stay with Marie, Mum wanted me back, not because she loved me but because she wanted to take her revenge, and the law was on her side. I had to accept that Dad had gone for good and I was going to have to live back home with Mum and my sister and four brothers, two of whom hated me as much as she did.

From the moment I walked through the door, a small boy needing to be comforted for his devastating loss, it was made clear that my place in the family was lower than that of any pet animal. I might have been Dad's favourite, but now I was loved by no one. My brothers were free to kick and punch and abuse me in any way they chose and there was nothing I could do about it. They used to eat at the table but I had to lick up the scraps they tossed on to the floor for me. I wasn't allowed to sleep in a bed, unless it was to allow my brothers to sexually abuse me and hurt me, but was relegated to the floor in a corner of the room with only a single blanket to cover me.

As the endless beatings and humiliations escalated, my throat and tongue seemed to close down, with the result that I started to stutter and gulp more and more, until eventually I was unable to speak at all, or even to make any sounds beyond tiny squeaks. When I cried, my tears ran silently down my face and no sobs escaped from my heaving chest. I had been silenced by the shock of what I had witnessed and could no longer beg for mercy or hope that I would ever be able to tell anyone about what was being done to me by my own family. I was trapped inside my own head.

Everything I did seemed to anger and disgust my mother and brothers even further, and the violence and abuse escalated with every passing month. They were constantly telling me how worthless and vile I was, and it became harder and harder to remember that Dad used to praise me and tell me how much he loved me. As the weeks turned into months, I started to believe the things they were telling me about myself: that I was beneath contempt and deserved to be hurt and demeaned all the time.

Eventually Mum could no longer bear to have me in her beautiful clean house any longer and I was dragged away and thrown into the dark, damp Victorian cellar with nothing but an old mattress to lie on and a bucket for a toilet. I sat in the darkness, dreading the threatening sound of approaching footsteps on the stairs even more than I dreaded the loneliness and hunger. Sometimes I would be left there for days on end without food or water, unable to call for help or beg for mercy, trapped inside my own silence, not even able to scream when they came down to beat or taunt me. In my head I would talk to Dad; I was able to see him sitting next to me in the gloom and able to hear his voice. It was my only comfort.

Things grew a thousand times worse when Amani became my mother's new lover. To me he seemed like a giant, ugly, alien figure. I heard that he came from Africa, but as far as I was concerned he could have come from another planet. My mother encouraged Amani to visit me in the cellar and relieve his sexual and sadistic needs whenever he chose. It started with him working off his sexual frustrations on me whenever he felt the urge, twisting my private parts painfully if I made any attempt to resist, and then he seemed to want to hurt me for the sheer pleasure of inflicting pain. He would rape me and then throw me aside, spitting on me and calling me names, as if it was all my fault and I was the dirty one. It seemed that to him I wasn't even human. The violence of his attacks and the force of his contempt for me seemed to amuse Mum and my brothers, reinforcing their own ideas of my worthlessness.

Only my eldest brother, Wally, ever showed me any kindness, sneaking down to talk to me whenever everyone else was out of the house, bringing me small shreds of hope that one day my nightmare would be over and telling me that it was Mum and Amani who were the bad ones, not us; but even though he was a young man by then, he was still too frightened of Mum ever to do anything about rescuing me or even speaking up in my defence. When he told me he was escaping from home to live with his girlfriend, I was sure he would tip the authorities off about where I was, but he never did.

It seemed as if the outside world forgot that I existed during those three years. Thinking back now, it's a miracle that I didn't die in that damp, airless, underground cell. If it hadn't been for the fact that I felt Dad was with me, willing me to keep going, I don't think I could have survived.

It wasn't until I was eight that the school authorities heard of my existence from my other brother, Thomas, and Mum was forced to bring me out of the cellar, still silent and frightened and struggling to cope with a world that seemed endlessly threatening and painful.

Chapter Two

Sold

Even once I was attending school like a normal child, my lack of a voice and my fear of the violence that I knew Mum, Amani and my brothers were capable of meant that I was still not able to escape the horrors of my home. While I was actually at school I was bullied and teased by the other children for being mute and backward and different, but nothing they could do to me was ever as bad as the torture I had already grown used to at home.

I still had to spend much of my life in the cellar when I was back in the house and as well as abusing me themselves, Amani and Mum decided that they could earn some money from me.

Amani had a contact, a man I only ever knew as Uncle Douglas, a seedy, overweight, evil-smelling old man who ran an organized paedophile ring from his home. At first when he was brought to the house I thought he was going to be nice to me, because he gave me sweets and wanted to take my picture, but when he tried to get my clothes off I fought back, biting like the little wild animal I had become, and he called Amani in to help him. The two of them raped and beat me together with all their adult strength, so that I would know it was never going to be worth fighting against them again, and so that I would understand that they expected me to be totally obedient, no matter what they demanded of me.

To begin with Mum sent me off with Uncle Douglas on my own to be 'groomed', which meant being repeatedly raped and abused in a hotel room deep in the countryside. He would drive me there, locked in the car, telling me of all the things that were going to happen to me and what the punishment would be if I tried to escape. He locked me into the boot of the car while he organized the room, only letting me out once the coast was clear for him to take me into the secluded, cabin-style room. Once I was safely in the room, he was free to beat and rape me and force me to perform any sexual act or humiliation that occurred to him. He took his time over everything, savouring the moment, even leaving me in the room, naked and chained to the radiator, while he went to the bar for a drink. There was nothing I could do because I had only the strength of a small child and I had no voice with which to call out for help.

Then Mum told me I was going to be a 'porn star'. Confident that he had broken my spirit and that I understood what I had to do, Douglas took me to his home. Children like me would be imprisoned there at weekends and during the school holidays, raped and defiled by a variety of men, every filthy act filmed and put on video. We were not allowed to speak to one another, or even allowed to make eye contact; we were treated just as slaves must have been 200 years ago.

The men who came to Douglas's house were monsters of cruelty, but they often looked like normal members of the public. There was no way of distinguishing them from the decent, kind people you find on every street. It was impossible for me to know who to trust and who to fear because everyone, particularly men, held the potential to be my tormentor. None of the other children I met in that house during those years had been abducted or kidnapped: they had all been introduced or sold to Douglas by someone from their own families.

Over the coming years I would meet so many young people on the streets and in the psychiatric wards of different cities who all had the same stories to tell of violence and rape, cruelty and betrayal at the hands of the people who should have been the ones protecting them from danger. No child starts out in life wanting to live rough on the streets or to develop an addiction to drink or drugs. It is always because of what has been done to them by others in the early years.

8

At school kind, well-meaning teachers and specialists worked at coaxing my voice back. Gently and slowly it returned, but the damage had already been done. I had lost three years of my life, which left me hopelessly behind the other children of my age in everything, and by then I was too brainwashed and terrified to ever give anyone even a hint of the sort of agony my life was at home. It was as if I inhabited two different worlds, one of which was a hell that would have been unimaginable to most of the other children who sat around me in classrooms.

When I was finally able to make myself understood, I made my first friend. Pete was a kind, clever and popular boy who took the time to listen to me and understand what I was trying to say. He liked me for who I really was and even took me home to his posh house to meet his parents. But in the end he was moved on to a better school than a seemingly backward child like me was ever going to be able to attend. He promised we would stay in touch, but I knew somehow that our friendship wouldn't last, and that I was going to be on my own again. Like Dad, he had been my protector and then he was gone from my life.

Chapter Three

Thrown Out

I was thirteen when I made my first bid for freedom, by just walking out of school and continuing walking until I was a safe distance away in the countryside. I managed to stay free for over a week before the police caught me. The thought of being sent back home to Mum and Amani terrified me, but I was even more frightened of grassing them up to the authorities. I fought as hard as I could to make the police believe me, telling them that my brothers abused me but not daring to mention Mum and Amani or Uncle Douglas. They had to investigate the accusations, which meant I had bought myself some more time, but the family all closed ranks and told the same story: that I was a liar and had been trouble from the day Dad had died. Mum was able to point to the accident as an explanation for why I had been struck dumb and why I was such a difficult and unstable child. She was always very good at persuading people in authority to believe her, which meant that none of them would have believed me even if I had had the courage to speak out.

In the end it was decided that there was no truth to any of my accusations about my brothers and I was delivered back home by the social services. The moment the social workers left, Mum and Amani reverted to their true characters and beat and raped me with even more violence than I had experienced until then. They were determined to break my spirit and ensure that I never thought about trying to run away again, but by then it was too late, because I now knew that it was possible to just walk away, even if my first attempt had ended in me being brought back. However much they hurt me and demeaned me when I was at home, they couldn't stop me from simply walking out of the door when I was back at school. I also now knew that there were places for children to run to and I bounced back and forth to a number of care homes once I was old enough to start running away from school and home, gradually being delivered back to Mum less and less often.

By that stage my head had been so messed with I was a real problem to anyone who tried to control me, even those who had good intentions and were hoping to help me. I was still too afraid to tell anyone the truth about what had been done to me throughout my childhood. The anger and fear and misery of the previous decade were stewing up inside my head and finally one day I flipped in the care home I was in at the time and exploded.

I was sixteen years old and I went on a wild rampage, smashing up my bedroom, not caring about anything any more, raging like a wild animal. The key workers tried to restrain me, but it was too late for that. My anger made me too strong for them and I managed to escape, running out of the home without having any idea where I was going. Once I was outside, I could see the rest of the staff having a meeting inside and I grabbed a brick, lobbing it through the window at them, shattering the glass and hitting one of them on the shoulder.

That night, when the police brought me back yet again, the man in charge of the home told me he'd had enough, and I was to leave.

'Pack your bags and get out,' he said, 'and don't come back.'

'I ain't got nowhere to go,' I snapped.

'Go back to your mother. You've got a home to go to.'

I knew Mum and the others had gone away for a few days and the house would be empty, so I slept in the garden shed for the night, planning what I was going to do next. I knew I had to leave the area and the only place I had ever heard of was Charing Cross in London. I'd heard other kids in the care homes talking about it after they had been caught and brought back, telling one another how great it was in the world of the homeless and free.

'Yeah, you've got to get away from this place,' they'd tell me. 'Charing Cross is the best place you could go to. There are millions of homeless kids there.'

Although I harboured the same wild dreams of becoming rich as most other young boys, it was the thought of finding someone to love, who would love me back, that was my greatest goal.

The next morning I broke into the house and went through it, collecting every bit of small change I could scrounge, as well as all the food and clothing I could find in the cupboards, stuffing it into my bag. There wasn't much there to take, as Mum squandered virtually every penny anyone brought into the house on drink, spending all her time down the pub and no longer cooking family meals for any of them. As I went, I left a trail of furious devastation behind me, smashing everything that came within reach, burning my bridges and making it impossible that I could ever return.

Chapter Four

Standing on the Slip Road

My heart was thumping as I stood by the side of the slip road down to the motorway at dawn. I was wearing my blue 'shell suit' and trainers – which was pretty much the only uniform I ever wore at the time – trying to thumb a lift down to London before anyone spotted me and took me back.

The adrenaline was still pumping from my rampage, the anger still throbbing in my head, and now I was anxious to get away from the area as quickly as I could, in case one of Mum's neighbours had heard the racket that I'd made when I was ransacking Mum's house, or seen me coming out and called the police to report the crime. Even in my agitated state I felt a bit guilty about all the damage I'd done, but at the same time I felt a strange sense of satisfaction at having finally taken a small revenge for all the pain that gripped my heart. I wanted it to be a final gesture to her and to my brothers and to Amani, before I disappeared from the area, losing myself for ever in the bustle and excitement that I was sure I would find in London.

I had all my worldly possessions, and whatever else I had been able to snatch from the house, in my precious bag. It was a sort of holdall backpack thing that was to become my closest and most treasured companion in the coming years. When you have practically nothing in life, you cling tightly to the few possessions you are able to truly call your own.

I was on a nervous high at the thought of finally escaping, like a freak burst of sheer happiness, which was helping me to cope with the cold of a spring morning and the steady drizzle that was soaking through to my bones, making my cheap clothes stick uncomfortably to my skinny, shivering frame and my hair hang lankly over my face. I must have looked a bit rough already, having slept the night in the shed before finally plucking up the courage to break into the empty house, and it had been at least an hour's walk in the rain to get to the slip road; so I suppose it wasn't surprising that the cars kept on streaming past and not even slowing down to consider offering me a lift. If I had been sitting inside a nice warm, dry, clean car, I probably wouldn't have wanted to stop in the rain and open my door to someone like me either.

It hadn't occurred to me for a moment during my walk to the slip road that I might not get picked up at all, but as the hours ticked past and the cars, vans, motor-bikes and lorries kept tearing by, most of the drivers not even giving me a second look, I felt fear gripping my guts with increasing intensity. What if I was left standing at the side of the road until a police car or someone who knew me came past and spotted me? What if they took me back and I had to face Mum and the rest of the family after I'd trashed her place and stolen her money? It might have been only a couple of quid in ten-pence pieces, but I would be judged on the principle of the thing, and the fact that I had dared to challenge her. I knew from past experience how immediate the punishment for even the smallest imagined transgression could be if she and Amani managed to get me on my own, and I could clearly picture what they would do to me for daring to make such a brave stand. I knew the authorities wouldn't take me back into the care home after I had lost my temper and hurled a brick through the window at them, so I couldn't expect any shelter there either. I had no option but to keep standing by the side of the road with my thumb out for as long as it took.

The hours kept on going by and the rain barely let up. My initial high spirits sank out of sight. After a whole day of being ignored, during which I took only the odd break to delve into my bag and eat the food that I had grabbed from the house, my feet aching from the standing around, a car full of young guys pulled up a few yards away from me. I felt my heart leap back to life with a mixture of relief, excitement and apprehension. Apart from wanting to get away from the cold and the wet, I was desperate to get out of sight and on my way, and finally my chance had come. Scooping up my bag, I ran towards the waiting car, my stomach tight with fear. I was always wary about climbing into cars with strangers, ever since Mum had sent me off with 'Uncle Douglas' in his car. I knew that once someone had you in a locked car you were trapped: you were their prisoner and they could pretty much do what they liked with you. I had no way of telling who were the potentially dangerous people amongst the world of strangers I was now entering; often in my experience it was the ones who were nicest to you at first who turned out to be the cruellest once they had you at their mercy.

I told myself it would be harder for people to overpower me now that I was sixteen and six foot tall, but the fear was too deeply embedded inside me to be susceptible to reason. I was tough, because I was ferocious like a cornered animal, but I was still just a boy and knew a determined man could easily beat me. The feeling in my stomach wasn't all fear. It was partly excitement too: excitement at the thought of starting a new life in a community of people like myself, people who would understand me and what I'd been through and wouldn't want to hurt me, people who had been abused and hurt and knew that the outside world could often be a kinder place than their own homes or the care homes they had been put into.

I believed that even if I had to sleep rough on the city streets I would still be part of a community, and there would be people coming round with food and blankets and all the basic essentials that I needed. Sleeping on the streets amongst friends would be infinitely preferable to anything that had happened to me in my life so far. It sounded free and adventurous, a million times better than being trapped alone in a cellar with no light or air or food as I had been for so many years, physically unable to speak to anyone. It was as if the kids in the care homes had been talking about a real never-never land – somewhere where kids like me could go to make our fortunes. When everything in your life is shit, you are eager to grab at any slim hope that there might be something better out there just waiting for you to discover it. If you didn't believe it, you wouldn't be able to keep going at all.

I could see the faces of the guys in the car watching me as I scooped up my bag and ran towards them, and they didn't look too bad. They were grinning and looked friendly. I put my hand on the handle of the door to open it just as it was ripped away from me with a screeching of tyres on the wet surface. The driver must have hit the accelerator all the way to the floor, and the car shot back on to the road and joined the rest of the traffic. I could see the guys' faces laughing back at me through the rear window and I knew they had planned this humiliation from the moment they had spotted me. They had seen someone less fortunate than themselves and decided to give me another kick just for the fun of it.

I felt the same boiling fury I had experienced when wrecking Mum's house rising back up inside me, but there was nothing and no one I could take it out on. Turning round and bending over, I yanked down my trousers and pointed my backside at my vanishing tormentors in a futile gesture of contempt. Even as I did it, I knew it was useless. What would they care that I had bared my arse at them like some ape at the zoo? It would just make them laugh all the more heartily, congratulating themselves on being the ones on the inside of the car amongst friends, not the sad loner left on the empty verge.

Pulling my cold, wet trousers back up, I collapsed on to the sodden grass and curled up into a tight ball to cry. At that moment it seemed as if that car had been my last chance of escape. It seemed as if I was never going to be allowed to get away and I was doomed to a sort of terrible limbo for all eternity. Everything poured out in those sobs. More than anything I blamed God, because who else could there be who could be so determined that I shouldn't be allowed to escape from the things and people that hurt me? What had I done to make Him so angry with me?

Because I had my head in my hands, I wasn't aware of the taxi approaching until I heard the engine coming to a halt beside me. I looked up to see what new tormentor I was going to have to deal with now. When I saw the light on the car, I was puzzled. Why would anyone think that I could afford a taxi?

'I didn't call a taxi, mister,' I said as the Asian driver climbed out and came round the car towards me.

'Are you all right?' he asked, looking as if he was genuinely concerned. 'Where are you going?'

'Charing Cross,' I replied, 'in London.'

'What's down in Charing Cross?' he asked.

'I've got family there,' I lied, worried that he would realize I was running away and would turn me in. Even though I was six foot tall I knew I looked and acted young for my age, and was obviously too young to be going to London on my own. 'I've got to hitch because I've lost my money.'

'Why don't you let me give you a ride?' he suggested.

'Listen, mate,' I said. 'I've only got two pounds and I don't want to be spending everything I've got on a taxi to London.'

If he thought it was funny that I was so ignorant I thought a journey of several hundred miles in a taxi would cost only a couple of pounds, he was too polite to show it. I'd never had money of my own before and so I had no idea really of the cost of anything. I imagined the handful of ten-pence pieces in my bag was going to last me for several days, until I got myself sorted out in some way.

'You can't stay here all night,' he said, gesturing towards the traffic speeding past. 'No one will stop for you in the dark, and then the police will come and pick you up. Let me take you to the station so that you can catch a train.'

'I told you, I had my money stolen.'

'I can lend you the money for a ticket.'

I was taken aback for a moment, suspicious of this unasked-for offer of kindness but tempted by it at the same time. Part of me longed to climb inside his warm dry taxi and get away from that bleak, exposed verge as quickly as possible. The other part of me feared a trap. I didn't want to get into a car on my own with a strange man. I had been caught too often that way before. But on the other hand he seemed a genuinely kind and gentle man, and he did have a proper taxi with a number and everything. After a few minutes of him cajoling and me snapping at him suspiciously, he managed to coax me into agreeing to go with him.

He opened the back door, but I could remember previous trips with Uncle Douglas or in police cars, and hearing the snap of the locks going down and not being able to get out, so I threw my bag on to the back seat, slammed the door and climbed into the front passenger seat as if I thought that was what he expected. He didn't seem bothered, hurrying round to the other side and climbing in. As he pulled out into the traffic, I stared straight ahead, trying to maintain a distance between us while I worked out what his game was. I had a clear plan in my head of what I would do to him if he showed the slightest sign of trying anything on with me.

21

Chapter Five

The Muslim Samaritan

As he drove me to the station, he told me his name was Mohamed and gave me a piece of mint-flavoured gum as he chatted. He seemed a nice man and I began to relax my guard a little as I chewed. I didn't like driving back into the city that I was trying to escape from, but I could see that he was right: I might never get away on the road. If he was genuinely willing to get me a train ticket, that was an offer I wasn't in a position to refuse. Arriving at the station, he parked in the taxi rank and we went in to the ticket office together, both of us unsure of how to behave with one another. The large, unsmiling woman behind the glass stared at us with a sort of unbothered hostility over the top of her half-moon glasses, like a headmistress trying to work out why a misbehaving pupil has been brought to see her.

'A single ticket for my friend to get the next train to London, please,' Mohamed said politely.

'They're doing repairs to the track,' she told him. 'Services have been suspended and he's missed the last connection to London for this evening.'

'When is the next connection, please?' Mohamed asked.

'Six o'clock tomorrow morning,' she said, looking past him and returning my angry, gum-chewing scowl with the calm stare of someone enjoying their little moment of power.

I could see that she was wondering what such a young-looking boy was doing travelling on his own and having his ticket bought for him by a middle-aged Asian man. It obviously struck her as strange. My heart was thumping and I was poised to run if she went to press an alarm button or pick up a phone to call the police. I felt so close to escaping, and the thought of having to hang around the cold station all night made me shiver. The disdain that she was showing towards Mohamed was stoking my anger back up again.

'Can I buy a ticket for tomorrow then?' Mohamed persevered.

'Are you travelling alone?' she asked me, ignoring him completely. 'Are you all right?'

'Course I'm all right,' I snarled back angrily. 'Look, woman, are you going to give us this ticket or not?'

All the boys in the homes I had been in talked like that to virtually everyone. We all wanted to sound like the black guys we met on the streets. We wanted to mimic their easy confidence and cheek in the face of authority. I expect we all sounded as foolish as Ali G suggested when he turned our patter into a comic character. I guess the ticket lady lost interest in my welfare at that moment, deciding I was a nasty piece of work and could look after myself for all she cared, because she passed the ticket over and took Mohamed's money.

'Enjoy your trip,' she said to me.

I glanced back as we walked away and saw that she was watching us go, obviously still curious about what our story might be, perhaps not certain that she had done the right thing by issuing the ticket. Maybe she had grandsons my age.

My next worry was how to get through a night on the station without being picked up by the police. I was still worried that Mum's neighbours might have reported the damage I'd done to the house, and once the police started checking me out they would pretty soon put two and two together. Thanks to Mohamed I now had my ticket to the promised land of Charing Cross; I just needed to stay out of sight for the next ten or so hours. I had a feeling that Mohamed had been as offended by the woman's suspicions as I had, but he didn't say anything as we walked back out to his taxi, both of us wondering what to do next. It was as if I had become his responsibility now.

'What are you going to do tonight, Joe?' he asked eventually.

'Find somewhere to wait, I suppose,' I said with a shrug, trying to look as if I wasn't bothered.

I guess he was worried about what would happen to me if he left me on the street, but equally he was nervous about giving the wrong impression by asking me if I wanted to go back to his place. We were both stuck in a strange, polite sort of limbo.

'Don't misunderstand me, please, Joe,' he said eventually, 'but why don't you come back to my flat for something to eat while you think about what to do next?'

All my instincts flared up and warned me to be wary. I knew from bitter and painful experience how foolish it could be to go to a strange place with a man I knew nothing about. But at the same time the option of being picked up by the police seemed worse. He appeared to be a genuinely kind man and he wasn't being pushy or creepy in any way. I decided it was a chance worth taking.

'OK,' I said, shrugging, as if it was I who was agreeing to do him a favour, rather than the other way round.

We climbed back into the car and as we drove I picked up a book that was lying next to the seat.

'What's this?' I asked, wanting to make conversation and break the awkwardness of the moment.

'It is the Qu'ran,' he said. 'The Holy Book. I am a Muslim.'

'That's where you're from?' I asked, having no idea what he was talking about.

25

'No,' he said, smiling. 'It is my religion. I am a Muslim Brother.'

My ignorance was so total that I stayed silent, unable to think what to say next without sounding stupid. He must have realized that I knew nothing and spent the rest of the trip trying to explain it to me. By the time we got to his flat I was lost in new thoughts as I tried to make sense of what he was telling me about his God and his beliefs. I liked the fact that he talked to me as if we were just friends, not like an adult with a difficult kid, which was the tone I was used to hearing in other people's voices.

'My wife and I are getting a divorce,' he explained as he opened the door to his flat. 'So I have only just moved into this place. Our marriage was arranged for us by our families and we were not suited. My family are all very angry with me for leaving.'

It was a cold, empty-feeling place with a musty, damp smell oozing from the shabby walls and worn carpet. There was hardly any furniture apart from a strangely old-fashioned record player housed in a wooden cabinet. There was no television or radio to break the silence of the little rooms. He explained that everything he owned he had left in the family house with his wife. The only decorations in sight were the pictures of the small children he had left behind in exchange for this bleak place. He saw me looking at the photographs and began to tell me about them, his face glowing with pride.

'You want to listen to some music?' he asked, gesturing towards the record player.

'OK.'

He pulled out an Elvis record and started dancing wildly round the flat, encouraged by my laughter to ever greater heights as he mimed to the words, eager to entertain me. I recognized the songs because my dad had been a big Elvis fan and used to play the songs in the car on the days when he drove me around to keep me out of Mum's way. The music was embedded in my head as firmly as the images of Dad burning to death in front of my eyes. It unlocked happy memories of our short time together but also reminded me of the cold horror of his love being snatched so cruelly away from me so young, the only love I had ever known.

When the song 'My Boy' came on, the surge of emotion took me by surprise. Images of my father and me together in the car, of sitting with him in the garage while he worked and of watching him running around in flames in front of me became overwhelming, and my laughter at Mohamed's wild antics turned to a choking sensation in my throat as I struggled not to cry. Dad used to play that song to me all the time, over and over again, telling me I was his boy. It was 'our song'.

The harder I fought to hold back the tears the more overwhelmed I felt by the emotions that the song unleashed in me. Mohamed stopped in the middle of his dancing, shocked to see that my tears of laughter had turned so suddenly to misery.

'What is the matter, Joe?' he wanted to know. 'Have you hurt yourself?'

'It's the song,' I said, not trusting myself to be able to explain any more than that.

'I'll turn it off. I'll turn it off.'

'No,' I said, not wanting to reject the memories of Dad and be left back in the awkward silence. 'I want to listen to it.'

'Not good song?' Mohamed asked, obviously worried that he had upset me.

'It's memories. My dad's song.'

As I listened to the rest of the track and cried, Mohamed stood beside me and put his hand on my shoulder until it was over.

'You want to listen to it again?'

'Yeah,' I nodded, no longer trying to hide the tears, wiping my running nose on my sleeve.

'I will go and make us some food while you listen,' he said, putting the track back on and disappearing out to the kitchen to leave me alone with my memories.

'No more Elvis,' Mohamed announced when he came back into the room a few minutes later. 'I am making us a nice curry.'

As the smell of cooking drifted into the room and my saliva glands started to work, I realized that I was really hungry. I had never tasted curry before, but I was ready for anything by the time he had managed to find a second chair to go beside the little garden-style table he had set up for us to eat from, and I dived straight in the moment he put the food in front of me, shovelling it into my mouth. The next moment I realized there was sweat breaking through every pore of my skin and my eyes were streaming with tears again, but for a different reason. It felt as if my mouth was on fire and I gulped water from the glass he had given me.

'Hot, hot, hot!' I gasped. 'More water.'

Mohamed giggled as he went out to get a jug. 'It is only a mild curry,' he said, laughing.

'You call that mild? It's taken the roof of my mouth off.'

He had given me a spoon to eat with, but he was tucking in himself with his hands, which shocked me. I had spent so many years forced to scrabble for scraps of food off the floor as a child at home that I couldn't understand why anyone would choose to eat like that and get their fingers so stained and sticky if they didn't have to. I certainly didn't intend to follow his example. If it could burn my mouth the way it had, I didn't want to risk burning my fingers too.

We were both easy in each other's company by then. He talked about his family and where he had come from and how he had arrived in England with his father. He tried to prompt me to talk about my life, but I didn't want to even think about it, let alone talk about it, and he didn't push me. I had also told him the lie about my family waiting for me in Charing Cross and I didn't want to give him any reason to think that he should try to stop me from running away from home. Now that he was becoming my friend I felt bad that I had told him lies. I had always been falsely accused of being a liar when I was a child and I hated the idea that now I was actually turning into one.

'The record "My Boy" – is that your dad's record?' he asked once we had finished eating.

'Yeah,' I said, and I could see that he was looking at me, waiting for me to go on. Reluctantly I told him about how Dad had died in the explosion in the garage he worked in, while I was sitting in the car watching, just five years old, but I didn't tell him anything about what had happened after that, once Mum got her hands on me and started to wreak her campaign of revenge, hiding me away from the outside world for years. I could see that he was shocked enough by what I had told him: there was no need to go any further. He stopped asking questions, not wanting to upset me any more. I could see that his eyes were beginning to glaze over with tiredness and I was certainly exhausted myself, but I wanted to put off the moment of going back on to the street for as long as possible.

'I can drop you back to the station now if you want,' he said eventually, 'or if you like I have a spare sleeping bag and you can sleep here for a few hours. I have no bed to offer you, I'm afraid.'

I could see that he was being very careful not to make it sound as if he was trying to take advantage, and I had also realized by then that there wasn't a bed anywhere in the flat. He hadn't given me any reason to distrust him and had shown me nothing but kindness.

'OK,' I said, as casually as I could manage. 'I wouldn't mind getting a few hours' sleep.'

'Good.' He seemed pleased that we had made a decision and bustled around clearing away the plates and folding up the table so that there was room for two sleeping bags on the floor. Almost the moment he put the light out I heard him start to snore.

Lying on a hard floor was not comfortable. Even at the worst of times, when I was locked in the cellar at home for days on end, I had still had an old mattress under me. But as I wriggled around trying to find a position I could sleep in, I was aware that I was going to have to get used to it, because once I got to London it was likely I was going to be sleeping rough for a while before I made my fortune or met the love of my life and managed to get a roof over my head.

Eventually I must have drifted off, because the next thing I knew it was half past four and Mohamed was nudging me up from a deep sleep, out of which I was very reluctant to pull myself.

'You must get train,' he said when I finally came to the surface enough to remember where I was and to make sense of what he was saying. At that moment all I wanted to do was slide back to the blissful oblivion of sleep, but Mohamed was being insistent. 'I make you a drink.'

He came back from the kitchen with a glass of orange squash.

'I will be back in a minute,' he said, disappearing out of the room again.

I drank the orange and got up to go to the bathroom. The door to the other room was ajar and I could see him down on his knees with his forehead touching the floor. I had never seen a Muslim at prayer before and had no idea what he was doing. It seemed to me that the whole world was populated by nutters, but at least Mohamed was harmless.

A few minutes later he came out and made me something to eat, and we set out for the station in the taxi. We arrived a few minutes early, so he came in to wait on the concourse with me. There were already crowds of passengers bustling around us, hurrying to get to their destinations. I felt a sense of apprehension building again, and was constantly shooting furtive glances around the station in case a policeman headed in our direction, or anyone who might recognize me.

'If you are ever in trouble, Joe,' Mohamed was saying earnestly, 'you must ring me.'

'OK.'

He wrote his name, address and telephone number down and passed it to me. I'm sure he must have guessed that I hadn't told him everything about my past or my plans for the future, and that there was something not quite right about the way that I was spiriting myself away from my home town. I assume most people knew that Charing Cross was a magnet to homeless kids in search of better lives than the ones fate had dealt them, but he was sensitive enough not to question my lies or try to stop me. Offering to be there for me should I need a friend was the best thing he could possibly have done for me, but I tried to make out it was no big deal. As I folded the piece of paper into my pocket, he gave me a wad of money.

'No, no,' I said, feeling that he had done enough for me, not wanting to be any more in debt to him than I already was.

'You repay me when you can,' he said, pushing it into my only partially reluctant hand. 'Send it in the post.'

Although I vowed to myself that I would do exactly that at the first opportunity, I expect he already knew that he would never see that money again. Once I got on the train I discreetly counted it and found he had given me £60, which was very generous for a man who was living in a bare flat and working every hour to try to support his ex-wife and children.

'You look after yourself,' he said, shaking my hand firmly. 'Be good and be strong.'

It seemed to me that he was a little tearful about saying goodbye. I wonder if perhaps he was as much in need of a friend at that moment as I was.

As I turned and trotted off to find the London train, I felt a renewed surge of excitement. I was nearly there, nearly free of the city where I had been imprisoned ever since the day my father died, and I was about to have a whole bunch of new experiences.

'Is this the train for London Paddington?' I kept asking anyone who would listen, no matter how many of them assured me it was. I had never been on a train before and I didn't want to risk getting on the wrong one, being whisked away to some other strange city and having to buy another ticket. I was mesmerized by the buzz of the station as the trains came and went and everyone else hurried around looking as if they knew exactly what they were doing and where they were going. I had no idea how far it was going to be from Paddington to Charing Cross; I just felt certain that once I was in London I would safe, able to melt into the anonymous crowd and leave the long agony of my childhood behind once and for all.

The London-bound train was surprisingly full. Maybe other people had had problems the previous evening like me but there were still quite a few seats in the carriage I chose. I settled down, looking all around me in awe, still nervously asking everyone if it was the right train. I was impressed by the space and comfort of the carriage, until the conductor came along and chucked me out, pointing out the signs on the window and the fact that I didn't have a first-class ticket. I answered back aggressively, as I always did when I felt threatened, but he was obviously more than experienced at dealing with my sort.

'Don't give me any more of your lip, lad,' he warned, and I stalked off with as much dignity as I could still muster.

The moment I passed out of first class I realized what a difference there was. There was none of the space and tranquillity in second class and by that time the carriages were crowded, and I only just managed to find myself a corner. It was only once I was wedged into the seat that I realized why it was still vacant. The man next to me smelled really badly of urine, like an old tramp. I pulled faces and made lots of comments to make sure no one thought it was I who smelled. Fortunately he got off a few stops later and I caught the eyes of the people opposite, pleased to see them laughing as I fanned ostentatiously under my nose.

The train was hurtling through the countryside, carrying me off to unknown adventures, and my spirits were soaring. I could hardly contain my excitement. Like a small boy at Christmas I was bouncing around, asking questions of anyone I could make eye contact with, making inane comments that I'm sure weren't anything like as funny as I thought they were. I was trying to make people have conversations with me when all they wanted to do was read their books or their papers, or catch up on some sleep after their early starts.

I just couldn't stop myself from rabbiting on and on, but no one wanted to hear from a scruffy little oik like me.

It was a while before I realized that everyone who came to sit near me during the trip eventually moved off to find another seat, but even once the penny dropped it didn't dampen my high spirits. I felt so free and so excited by the adventures that I was sure now lay ahead of me.

Chapter Six

Never-never Land

We pulled into Paddington station around lunchtime and I strolled out into the streets of London, amazed to think that I was now in the famous city that I had heard so much about and that I was free to wander wherever I chose without having to worry about who I might bump into. It felt as if I had travelled all the way to the other side of the world.

One of the people I had been babbling to on the train had told me I was going to have to get 'the Tube' to Charing Cross. This was another new concept I was having trouble getting my head around. Was I really going to be able to travel under the streets and buildings in a train? I looked around, trying to work out where I should go next. I had never seen so many people rushing around in different directions at once. The level of activity all about me took my breath away. I tried to ask several people to help me find the right entrance to the right line for Charing Cross, but no one even paused or caught my eye – they were all so busy going about their business, bumping into me every time I paused to try to work out what I should be doing and where I should be going.

Maybe they were worried I was going to ask them for money or would try to steal something off them.

Eventually I found the entrance and went underground, but there were still signs to different lines and I didn't know which ones to follow. There were maps on the walls, but my reading skills were not the most brilliant and the complexity of the diagrams made my head spin. I began to feel panicked and kept plunging around asking people for help until I found someone willing to spare me a few seconds of their valuable time. After what seemed like an age I found myself crushed on an underground train, hurtling along through tunnels in completely the wrong direction, having no idea how I would get back out again through the crowd when I reached the next station. I felt as if I was trapped in a nightmare, becoming disorientated and frightened and wondering how I would ever find this wonderful place that the other runaways had told me about. So far I hadn't seen anyone who looked as if they were likely to be living like me, or who would want to be my friend.

Every time the train stopped I would ask if the station was Charing Cross and someone would shake their head. I couldn't work out whether I was getting closer to my destination or further away, but eventually a woman told me that I was there, and I jumped out on to the platform quickly before the doors had a chance to snap shut and carry me away in the wrong direction again. The station was called Embankment, not Charing Cross, but a man in uniform assured me I was in the right place and showed me which exit to go through.

I think I expected to walk straight out and see a paradise of young homeless people all hanging out together around camp fires built amongst makeshift cardboard homes; but as I came out into the daylight, just across the road from the Thames, the street seemed to be like any other busy city street, with everyone dashing about, trying to get to somewhere important. There was a small park with a bandstand on one side, behind some railings, but I couldn't see anyone in there who looked like me either, and in the other direction there were some railway arches, which merely led to another street full of rushing traffic. Apart from the people manning the flower stall, or selling the evening papers from metal stands, everyone else was moving about purposefully between the Tube and what I soon discovered was the mainline station at the top of the hill.

Where was this community of carefree runaways that I had been led to believe would be there to welcome me into their arms? There was no option other than to tramp around the streets to see if I could find some secret entrance to this world I had come searching for.

I started walking, looking round every corner for one of these places where I had heard a homeless boy could find a meal or pitch a bed, but I couldn't see anything. All the shops in the Strand were brightly lit and full of people spending money. None of them seemed as if they would welcome someone as scruffy and disreputable looking as me, so I stayed on the outside, staring in. I still couldn't see any homeless people anywhere, just normal citizens going about their daily business, all of whom I assumed would be returning to their homes and their comfortable beds in a few hours. What was I going to do then, when the streets were suddenly empty? Was I just going to have to huddle down on my own in one of these shops' doorways once the staff had pulled down the shutters and gone home? Or should I go round the back of the buildings and see if I could find an air vent which would provide me with a bit of warmth against the night air?

I had probably been walking for an hour or more before I came across a lad who looked about my age and was sitting on the pavement begging off passers-by. He was scrawny and rough looking, but his clothes looked as if they had once been better than mine, although they were now dirty and worn. He had a young, pretty-boy's face but his expression was furtive, like that of a wary little wild animal, poised to either attack or run. He didn't look like someone who could be trusted. He was sitting on a sheet of cardboard with a sleeping bag over his lap and a pot in front of him, holding up another piece of cardboard scrawled with the one word 'home-less'.

'Spare any change?' he asked as I drew near, staring at him curiously.

There was no way I was going to give him any money, being sure I was going to need every penny of the sixty quid that Mohamed had given me in order to survive, but I still wanted to strike up a conversation with him.

'I'm homeless too,' I said by way of an apology as much as an explanation.

'What do you mean?' he demanded, seeming quite angry despite his soft way of talking. To me he sounded quite well spoken, as if he was more educated than me, but maybe it was just a regional accent I was unfamiliar with. 'You look all right to me.'

'Just telling you,' I said.

'How long have you been here?'

'I've just arrived and I don't know no one.'

He looked exasperated, as if he knew I was one more stupid kid expecting pavements of gold and not know-ing what to do next now that I had actually arrived.

'Sit down then,' he said, gesturing to another grubby sheet of cardboard beside him while he continued to hold his sign up at the passers-by, most of whom ignored him. 'Spare some change?'

In between begging, he told me his name was Jake, and once he'd got used to the idea he seemed to like teaching a newcomer the rules of the street. He told me that I should avoid the police because they would have me down at the police station in a van if they could get hold of me, and then I would be shipped straight back to where I had come from.

'You need to stick with the same bunch of people all the time,' he explained, 'because that way you'll be protected from the rest.'

I had heard from other runaways about how homeless kids got together into little social pods for self-protection. I liked the idea of being a member of a gang instead of always being on my own.

'So where do I meet these people?' I wanted to know.

'You have to be careful,' he warned. 'They get quite funny with new people coming in. They'll see you as an outsider and they won't want to take responsibility for new people.'

I must have looked a bit crestfallen.

'You'd better stay with me for now,' he said, 'and we'll go from there.'

All the time we were talking he was shaking his pot at people and asking for change. I was surprised how many of them actually gave him something and every so often he would empty most of the contents of the pot into his pocket and then go back to shaking and asking. One or two people would annoy him by refusing to give him anything and he would get quite cheeky with them, which made me nervous. I didn't like the idea of attracting the outside world's attention if I could avoid it – not till I knew my way around a bit better. He told me about the outreach centre, which was a project for the homeless run by volunteers, where I could get something to eat and some warmer clothes and a blanket for the night.

'They'll give you a list of hostels if you want and if they aren't full. You can have a shower there, too, and clean yourself up a bit. I'll take you there now.'

But when we got there we found it was closed for the night. Jake didn't seem bothered and just started introducing me to a group of homeless people who were sitting around outside the centre, killing time. If you have no home and no job and no family, killing time is pretty much all you ever do.

Now that the city workers were beginning to disappear off the streets and into the stations, it became easier to see the homeless community that they left behind. A lot of the people Jake knew appeared to be paired off in boy–girl relationships, which seemed a bit strange to me. They were a bit like a normal group of young people meeting up of an evening and having a few drinks together, except they were doing it in the street rather than in a bar or a pub. It wasn't what I had been expecting, but the pairing off was encouraging because that was what I wanted: a nice girlfriend who I could love and be loved by, someone who would understand me and always be there for me and who I could look after.

Everyone seemed to recognize Jake, which made me think he must have been living on the streets for a while and knew his way around, but I got the feeling they didn't particularly respect him. The first people were a bit wary of me, but then he found a group who were more relaxed. There was a lad they called Jock, although I think that was just a nickname given to him because he was Scottish, not his given name. He was older than Jake and me, probably eighteen or nineteen years old, and seemed to be really wised up to everything, as if he was a sort of leader amongst the rest of them. He looked even older than his years because his teeth had already started to rot – not that mine were too clever at that stage, since I'd never been near a dentist and had suffered from malnourishment for most of my life. After Dad died I wasn't allowed to see daylight most days, let alone be taught how to use a toothbrush. Jock and his friends seemed happy for me to hang around with him and so his other friends automatically accepted me. I had found a gang I could be part of and I started to relax and enjoy the adventure.

As we all strolled from one place to another, as normal teenagers might wander from one person's house to another or from one pub to the next, we talked all the time. They all asked me questions about my past and initially I was a bit cagey, always finding it hard to talk about how I had been treated by Mum and my brothers and all the men who she had sold or given me to. It seemed like a shameful and humiliating thing to have had happen to me, and anyway I didn't like to think about it.

'My dad used to rape me all the time,' one girl told me, shocking me with the ease with which she found she could talk about it but at the same time making me feel good that I wasn't the only one such things had happened to. It was almost as if it was something normal for her. As the hours passed and I listened to more and more of their stories, I realized that many of them had had similar experiences. As the evening wore on and the drink eased my tongue, I opened up more and more. I started by telling them about Dad burning to death in front of me and about how much he had meant to me, being my champion and my hero and my protector, and how his death had left me dumb and unable to speak for years. That story got a shocked reaction, but when I went on to tell them how Mum had locked me in the cellar for years they were truly amazed.

'What?'

'You're joking, man.'

'I couldn't have handled any of that.'

'That's so unreal,' a girl called Charlotte said. 'I always thought my mum was a bitch but she never did anything like that.'

They kept pumping me for more stories and once I realized they weren't going to judge me it was a sort of relief to actually put into words the things I had been storing up in my head for so long, suffering so much pain as a result. It was as if it was no big deal to any of them, even though it was shocking, and we were all there together to talk and support one another.

'Have you got any money on you?' someone asked. 'Because we need to buy some booze.'

My guard immediately went back up again. There was no knowing how long I was going to have to survive on the wad of notes Mohamed had given me. I could see that if I owned up to having it now it could all be spent within a few hours and I would be left with nothing. I was keeping a hold on my bag as if my life depended on it and when someone started trying to rummage around in it I snatched it away.

'We share everything here,' someone said.

'That's my property,' I insisted. 'It's private.'

On my search through Mum's house before leaving I had managed to find my birth certificate, which I had never seen before and somehow knew was going to be important to me, and also my dad's watch, which I knew he would have wanted me to have and which was all I had left of him. I don't know why Mum had even kept it, considering how much she hated him for leaving her – perhaps she thought she would sell it one day. Sometimes, when I felt unsure of myself, I would just hold it for comfort, as if I was holding my dad's hand. Sometimes I would talk out loud to him, just as I had done in my head when I had been on my own in the cellar in the dark, which made other people think I was talking to myself. I guess they thought I was a bit touched in the head, and maybe I was.

Realizing that I was willing to fight to protect my possessions, the others backed off, but then I felt mean and guilty for lying because they all started rummaging around in their own bags and pockets, finding bits and pieces of food which they shared with me.

As it grew darker, we continued to move around in a group, trying to keep warm, talking and laughing all the time, sometimes shouting out to people as the drink made us bold and foul mouthed. I was surprised by how many people were still coming and going from the stations on their way to theatres, hotels and restaurants in the Strand, or maybe some of them were on their way home after working shifts. I hadn't realized that big city life went on so late, and I liked the buzz and the constant distractions. It made me feel safe to have people around, even though they were strangers and could for all I knew have been predators. I knew from experience that some of the most perverted and heartless men looked completely normal and respectable on the surface, often well dressed and sporting wedding rings. Any one of the men walking past could have been the sort of man who visited the places where I had been kept as a child and continuously raped and abused.

We went on asking for change from everyone we passed, but no one handed any over, probably because they could see we were drinking and guessed that was what we wanted the money for. The others were becoming quite loud and intimidating, which was making me uneasy, but I didn't want to leave the group and end up on my own. I felt that at least Jock and the others offered me a little protection against the rest of the world. I wanted to belong.

Everyone living on the streets in that area seemed to know Jock, not just the kids but the old winos as well, and they would call out to him as he passed, or come over to pay their respects, offering to share their cans of cider or whatever they had.

'Jake!' a voice called from across the Strand. 'Come over here.'

I looked across and saw a man in an old Mercedes, which had pulled up at the kerb. Even in the dark he looked sinister and swarthy, much older than anyone in our group. There were two other guys in the back of the car, but I couldn't see them clearly.

'It's Max,' Jake said, and I thought he looked nervous suddenly.

'Don't fucking go to him, you fucking idiot,' Jock snarled, holding him back.

'No, Jock, I've got to go,' Jake said, wriggling free.

'Oh, fuck off then.' Jock pushed him away angrily. 'Go be Max's bum-chum.'

I watched as the man they called Max got out of the car to talk to Jake. He was tall and rangy and looked strong. I could see tattoos creeping up his scrawny neck from his collar. He looked dangerous and I felt a shiver of apprehension. Max opened the back door of the car and Jake jumped in with the other guys without glancing back at us. It was as if the car swallowed him up, the doors snapping shut like jaws.

'Fucking idiot.' Jock spat and took a swallow from his can as the Mercedes drew away and disappeared towards Trafalgar Square.

'Let's get something to eat,' he said, leading the way to what I assumed would be a café or takeaway.

'I've got no money, Jock,' I reminded him, not able to admit to my secret store of notes now I had denied having them.

'You don't need money here, mate,' Jock said, laughing at my naiveté. 'It's all free. It's a soup kitchen.'

The homeless centre was open again, and the volunteers provided us with stew and bread and hot tea in plastic mugs. I ate as if I hadn't seen food in a year, hardly able to believe that I could have as much as I wanted and all for free. The meal raised my spirits again as it warmed my insides. I was having an adventure in London with a group of new friends and no one to tell me what to do, and now I had a full stomach as well. Charing Cross really was turning out to be the homeless paradise I had been told about. The volunteers were offering blankets to anyone who wanted them, but I felt quite warm again now I'd eaten and I didn't want to have to carry anything else around with me as well as my bag.

Chapter Seven

A Confused Boy

ack out on the streets we started hunting behind the buildings, riffling through the big metal bins that were being put out by the shops, hotels and restaurants, and searching for anything that might be useful or that we might want to eat if we got peckish later that night. I didn't really know what I was looking for, so I just followed everyone else's lead. The stores were the best places: they threw out food that was a day past its sell-by date but still perfectly good. As it got colder I pulled out of my bag all my spare clothes, which were only a couple of jumpers and another pair of trousers, and put them on over what I was already wearing. I must have looked a right sight, but I didn't care, because at least I was warm and I knew none of the people I was with were making any judgements about my appearance – they were well past the stage of even noticing.

The others were also collecting up any flattened cardboard they could find, opening it back up to rebuild the boxes, which must have been used to deliver goods to the shops earlier in the day. Everyone was calling out to one another, competing to see who could find the best box. I wasn't as quick as the others and didn't really know what I was looking for, so by the time I realized that what I needed was something I could sleep in for the night, I only had something tiny.

Once everyone had what they needed, we wended our way back down to the park, which was now finally empty of other people and filling up with an eerie, makeshift city of cardboard as everyone set about constructing themselves some sort of shelter for the night, covering them with plastic to protect them from the damp that was bound to descend before morning.

Everyone was huddled in the small groups that they had been in all evening, avoiding encroaching on the territory of anyone else who might be angrier, more violent and more drunk than they were, and staking a claim to a patch of land that was going to be theirs for the night. As everyone got settled, the odd fistfights would break out when one group felt that another had crossed over their boundary, and there were a few squabbles for the best, most sheltered sites.

Gradually, as exhaustion and alcohol took their toll, people began to fall asleep, pulling blankets and sleeping bags up over their heads and disappearing from the world for a few hours. As we all crawled into our shelters, the sounds of shouting and fighting become more intermittent as more people surrendered to sleep. Every so often a policeman or two would wander past the park, but they didn't seem to be too bothered about anything that was going on. I guess it was easier for them to have all the homeless people corralled behind railings in one area than to have them curled up in shop doorways and back alleys all over the place, causing complaints from local residents and shopkeepers when they came to open up in the morning.

I managed to get my box together and put some plastic over it as the others showed me, but when I came to lie down it was impossible to curl all six foot of me into it, so I had to leave my legs sticking out, using my bag as a pillow with the handles looped round my wrist to make sure no one nicked it in the night.

Jake arrived back from wherever he had been with the man in the Mercedes and didn't have any trouble finding us. He had picked up some cardboard for himself on the way.

'What you doing with that box?' he said, laughing, when he saw my legs sticking out. 'You don't fit in it.'

'The others got the best ones.'

'You've got to be faster than that, mate.'

'Where have you fucking been, Jake?' Jock growled from near by in the dark.

'I had to do something for Max,' Jake said, obviously not wanting to talk about it.

'That fucking bastard! Why do you do whatever he tells you?'

I didn't understand why Jock felt so strongly about this Max guy, but I was too tired to ask any more questions. Now that I was no longer moving about to keep warm, I was regretting not picking up one of the blankets at the centre. The others had put up another plastic sheet and tied our boxes together so that when it started to rain most of the water could be kept off us, but I was still feeling cold and damp. I would organize things better the next day, I told myself as I dozed off, now that I knew what was needed. Things would get steadily better from here on – I was confident of it. I could still hear the odd raised voice in the distance but it didn't bother me any more; I felt safe enough to sleep. Here and there muffled giggles came from other boxes, and the sounds of couples having sex.

It must have been just after midnight when I was woken by the sound of voices.

'Hello? Hello? Come on. We're here. Hello? Does anyone want blankets?'

That was exactly what I needed, so I wriggled out of my box to see what was going on. A middle-aged woman was standing outside with her arms full of old-looking blankets, passing them out to anyone who asked.

'Do you want something to eat?' she asked as I went over to her. 'The van's just over there.'

I looked over to where she was pointing and saw a van parked outside the Tube station, with a table set up beside it doling out soup and rolls to warm us up.

'Come on,' she said, putting a blanket round my shoulders. 'It's a cold night. Wrap up well. We need to look after you. You're a new face. My name's Sarah. What's yours?'

'Joe.'

'Come on then, Joe.'

She took me over to the van with the blanket round my shoulders and gave me some soup. Jock came ambling over and she obviously knew him well.

'You've been drinking again, Nigel,' she said, wagging her finger at him. 'Haven't you?'

I looked up in surprise, startled to find out this hard man's real name. Jock did not look like a 'Nigel' to me.

'I wouldn't do that, Sarah,' he said, grinning like a little boy being told off by a popular teacher.

'Don't you tell me any of your fibs, Nigel. How old are you then, Joe?' she asked.

'I'm sixteen,' I said, more aggressively than I probably should have done, but I was fed up with people thinking I was younger.

'Are you sure?'

"Course I am, you mad woman.'

'Oh, now,' she clucked. 'I don't want to upset you, lovey. How long have you been here?'

I was getting tired of all the questions and said nothing. I just wanted to get some soup inside me and go back to my cardboard box for more sleep.

'Is anybody looking after you?' she asked, looking across at Jock as she spoke.

'Yes,' Jock sighed. 'I'm looking out for him.'

'You make sure you do, Nigel. He looks very young to be down here. Who else have you met?' she asked me.

'Jake.'

'Oh,' she said, pursing her lips. 'The less said about him the better.'

Just at that moment Jake came stumbling over for his soup and I could see she was trying to pack him off back to the boxes again as quickly as possible so that she could get back to talking to Jock and me.

'Keep Joe away from him, Jock,' she said once Jake was out of earshot. 'That boy is confused. And that Max! You stay away from him, Joe, or he'll get you into a lot of trouble.'

'I fucking told him today, Sarah,' Jock assured her.

'You keep him in your sight all the time, Nigel. And don't let Jake anywhere near him.'

I felt comforted by this kindly woman's obvious concern for my safety, but at the same time her words of warning worried me. I had met enough violent and dangerous men during my childhood to know that I didn't want to meet any more. Standing in the middle of a strange city in the dark and cold made me feel suddenly vulnerable, and anxious to hurry back to my box so that I could curl up under my blanket to hide from the world until morning. I moved off but found Sarah was coming with me.

'Is that your box?' she asked, obviously horrified.

'Yeah,' I said. 'It's OK.'

'For goodness sake!' She turned to Jock. 'Nigel, find Joe a decent-sized box. He can't sleep in that little thing.'

'He can have mine,' Jock muttered grudgingly, wandering off to find himself something else while Sarah settled me in and made sure I was as comfortable as I could be, like a mother tucking in her child even though he was too old for such attention. It was an experience I had certainly never had with my own mother and I didn't know how to react to it. She took no notice of my protests that I wasn't a kid. By the time she had finished, every part of me was as warm as toast apart from my nose.

The next time I woke up it was morning and Jock had already disappeared. I felt a momentary lurch of anxiety at having lost my protector, but I knew I couldn't really expect him to look after me just because some mad old woman had told him to in the middle of the night. Jake was the only one of our group still around.

'Where have they all gone?' I asked.

'Up the centre. Want to come?'

Although Sarah's warnings about Jake were still ringing in my ears, I didn't think I had any choice, unless I

wanted to stay in the park on my own. The park workers were already starting to clear away the cardboard
debris of our almost abandoned camp. I decided any
company was better than none and went with him. As
we made our way through the streets, I became aware of
a car drawing up beside us and I recognized the old
Mercedes I had seen Jake getting into the previous
evening. Jake stopped as the man I now knew was Max
got out and came round to talk to him.

'Hiya, fella,' Max said to me. 'You all right?'

'Yeah,' I nodded cautiously.

There was something about this man that told me I
shouldn't give him any cause to get angry. I noticed the
big gold sovereign rings on his fingers, and he had the
words 'love' and 'hate' tattooed on his knuckles, as well
as the illustrations I had already noticed on his neck.

'Do you need any money?' he asked.

I couldn't understand why he would be offering
money to someone he didn't even know. Then I remembered how Mohamed had given me money for nothing
and told myself not to be so suspicious, and that maybe
people were nicer than I had been led to believe by my
childhood experiences. I took the fiver he was offering
and slid it into my pocket.

'If you need anything, you come and see me,' he said
with a wink that should have seemed friendly but didn't.

* * *

The following days fell into a routine. We would go to the centre in the morning to get something to eat and have a shower. The volunteers there were always really good with us and helpful. There was a doctor there each day, who checked us over and gave us prescriptions if we needed them. I had always had trouble with asthma, so they gave me a prescription for an inhaler. It was nice to know there was someone to go to if I got ill. Then we would wander out into the streets, buy something to drink and drift around from place to place getting pissed and begging, going back to the centre for an evening meal and then settling down under whatever cardboard we had been able to find for another night. I never needed to touch the money in my bag because everything was provided or could be bought with the change that people gave us.

I frequently ended up spending most of my time with Jake because Jock and his girlfriend, Charlotte, were always drunk and stoned and hanging out with the tramps and winos around the Strand, while Jake and I didn't want to be doing that the whole time. Charlotte was a really pretty girl and I never worked out what she was doing with Jock and the other losers. Jake and I got bored with their company quite often and wanted to see different things and different places, so we would go off begging together. Jake knew all the different outreach centres where we could get food through the day and my initial wariness after Sarah's warning faded as I got used to him. He seemed pretty harmless to me. It wasn't such a bad life, I told myself: better than being locked in a cellar and continually beaten up and raped, and better than being in a care home with everyone bossing you about and treating you as if you were some kind of problem.

Some nights Jake would disappear and not turn up again till the following morning.

'Where have you been?' I'd ask.

'Oh, I just stayed at Max's for the night,' he would say, obviously not interested in saying any more.

I'd been in London for a week and a second weekend had come round when Jake told me that Max had asked to have a word with me, to check that I was OK. I wasn't that keen, but I remembered he had been friendly and given me a fiver the last time we had spoken, so there didn't seem to be any reason to worry about it too much. It was broad daylight in a busy street anyway, so what could happen?

'Why's he so interested?' I asked.

'He's just worried about you,' Jake said, shrugging. 'Because you're a bit young he wants to check that you're OK.'

The Mercedes pulled up beside us again as it had before and I saw that there was another guy with Max, who looked like a minder, with an evil fighter's face that had taken a few punches over the years. They told me his name was Brad.

Max greeted Jake effusively and handed him a bunch of cash. 'That's for the other night,' he said, patting him on the back as if they were the best friends in the world. The previous times I had seen Max he had been dressed smart casual, as if he was going out somewhere. This time he was just wearing trackie bottoms and looked more relaxed, as if he had just got out of bed.

'How are you doing, fella?' he said, turning his unconvincing charm on to me.

We chatted for a bit and then he turned back to Jake.

'Fancy coming back to the flat for a bite to eat?'

'We're just going to the soup kitchen,' I said.

'Oh, that's fucking horrible food,' Max said. 'Come back and have something to eat with us. I'll drop you back – don't worry.'

The threatening look of the minder as he got out of the car brought Sarah's warning words back to me. But at the same time I was nervous that if I said no they would be insulted and get angry. They hadn't done anything bad to me – quite the opposite – so what right did I have to judge them just because they looked a bit rough? And I did fancy a decent meal. I was torn in my mind, and in that moment of indecision the minder opened the back door of the car and I panicked.

'No,' I said. 'I don't want to go in the back. No way.'

'That's all right, fella,' Max said. 'You can sit in the front next to me.'

He opened the passenger door and I allowed myself to be steered into the seat. The minder and Jake got into the back and everyone chatted away as we drove across London. They were so friendly I felt my fears settling and I began to feel foolish for making such a fuss and being so suspicious of their motives. I started to look forward to having a decent meal.

Chapter Eight

Max's Flat

We drove for about half an hour and pulled up outside a big grey block of council flats, the sort with open concrete walkways on every floor leading from one front door to the next past windows shrouded in net curtains, protected by metal bars or boarded up.

'Maybe we should get back,' I said to Jake as I stared up at the forbidding, bleak-looking buildings.

'Don't be stupid,' Jake said, avoiding my eyes. 'Let's at least have something to eat. I'm hungry.'

'It's OK, fella,' Max said, obviously able to see how nervous I had become again. 'No one will try to hurt you. If they do, I'll beat them up for you.'

He and Brad led the way without bothering to look back, laughing and talking together as if they were confident we would follow. Realizing that I had no idea how to get away from the area on my own anyway, I took a deep breath and went after them, clutching my bag tightly to me, sure I was going to be mugged despite Max's assurances and even though there didn't seem to be anyone around. Max and Brad were being so friendly and they weren't trying to force me to go with them, and Jake seemed perfectly happy with them, so why was I being so fearful? I told myself to stop being paranoid. I couldn't let my past experiences make me frightened for ever.

We climbed some concrete stairs past walls covered in aggressive-looking graffiti and went along one of the walkways until we reached a black front door with a glass panel in the top. The bottom panel had been boarded over, as if someone had kicked the glass in. Max let us in. As I walked into the front room I could smell a sweet, smoky aroma, which I later discovered was cannabis. There were two guys on a sofa, sucking smoke up from a hubble-bubble, both giggling and stoned.

'Hi, Jake,' they called out when they saw him. 'Come here.'

Jake went over and they were hugging and kissing him, which I thought was a bit odd, ruffling his hair and being really mellow and friendly. I began to relax a little, despite the unfamiliar surroundings. They encouraged me to take a suck of the smoke, which was the first time I had ever done it. I didn't even smoke cigarettes and I nearly choked as it burned into the back of my throat, making the others fall about laughing like hyenas at my discomfort. They encouraged me to take hit after hit, assuring me I would get used to it soon. As I became high, I felt a bit dizzy and had trouble protesting when Max offered to take my bag off me so that I could be more comfortable, so I just clung on to it as tightly as I could. The cannabis was making me feel strangely calm and accepting of everything that was happening. I found myself chattering away as if they were my oldest friends in the world. They brought me some food, but I wasn't hungry, feeling a bit sick from the smoke.

'So,' Max said, 'do you like to earn money, Joe?'

Shocked by the suddenness of the question, I tried to muster my drifting thoughts into some sort of order; I was fearful that if I wasn't careful I would commit myself to doing something I might later regret.

'Yeah,' I said, cautiously. 'I suppose so.'

'You want a job?'

I thought perhaps he needed someone to clean the flat or something. It looked as if it needed it. 'Yeah.'

'What would you be willing to do for it?' he asked.

'Anything,' I said, not bothered by how hard or demeaning the job might be, knowing that beggars couldn't be choosers in the jobs market. I had to start somewhere, after all.

'Anything? Right. Would you sleep with a woman?'

Even to my befuddled brain that sounded like an odd question. 'Course I would.'

'Ah.' He nodded wisely. 'Would you sleep with a man?'

The moment his words penetrated my consciousness alarm bells went off inside my head and I doubled my efforts to sober up and concentrate on what was going on. In a second I was transported back to the vile house that Uncle Douglas used to take me to for days on end, locking me in with the other kids and forcing us all to do the most disgusting things with the men who came to the door, beating us if we dared to protest or refuse, or even to make eye contact or speak before we were spoken to. For a horrible moment I wondered if Max was one of the people who liked to watch the films that Uncle Douglas and his friends had made of us. Was that why he was asking these questions? Had he seen me being raped and believed I'd enjoyed it? I realized now that Max had the same air about him as Douglas and his friends. That was why he had made me so uneasy from the start; that was why he had made me feel so afraid before I even knew why. The other guys in the room just kept on bonging as if they couldn't hear the conversation, or as if it was the most normal thing in the world to be discussing when we hardly even knew each other. They were far too stoned to be able to help me, even if they had wanted to.

'No,' I said. 'I wouldn't sleep with a man.'

'Why not?' He pretended to be surprised by my answer, as if it was stupid or something.

'I don't do that,' I said, trying not to let the fear I was feeling affect my voice. I wanted to stay in charge. I had to or else I would be a helpless kid again, as I had been for the previous ten years or more of my life. 'I'm not gay.'

'It's got nothing to do with being gay,' Max said. 'It's about earning money, boy. You can earn good money with me. I've got your friend Jake here. He doesn't mind sleeping with men.'

Jake was either too stoned to notice what was going on or deliberately avoiding looking at me.

'I've gotta go now,' I said, struggling to get to my feet, willing my legs to stop wobbling beneath me. It didn't matter how threatening the estate outside might look: I could see now that this flat was where the real danger lay. I remembered Sarah's warnings my first night on the streets, telling me to steer clear of Jake and Max. She must have known all about this. I realized now why Jake disappeared during the night so often: he was on the game and Max was his pimp. That was why Jock hated Max so much. I wished Jock and Sarah had explained things to me more clearly. I would never have made the stupid mistake of getting into Max's car if I had known what he was into. This was my worst nightmare, the very reason I had run away from home in the first place. I couldn't believe I had been so stupid and naïve. The moment I got unsteadily to my feet Max pushed me back down and I toppled over on to the sofa.

'You're staying,' he told me. 'You're in my house now and I'll tell you when you are going to leave. I've got a punter coming round. He wants to see you.'

I wasn't sure what a 'punter' was, but it didn't sound good.

'I'll show you to your room now,' he said.

'No,' I shouted. 'I want to go.'

'I'll show you your fucking room,' he said again and there was no mistaking the menace in his voice. He grabbed my skinny arm so tightly with his giant hand that it made me squeak from the pain as he lifted me bodily off the sofa, propelling me towards the door, still clutching my bag. The more I struggled the tighter his grip became, his fingers digging in.

'Just do what I fucking tell you,' he hissed into my face. 'Don't be fucking disrespectful.'

'It's all right, mate,' Jake slurred from the depths of the other sofa. 'Don't worry.'

'I want to go,' I screamed, the panic overwhelming me and making my voice hysterical.

As Max dragged me through to the bedroom, I noticed there was a key in the lock on the outside and my panic doubled as every memory of being imprisoned rushed back. Once I was past that door they would be able to keep me there for years and there would be nothing I could do about it, just as it had been with Mum and the men at home. I fought and struggled with all my strength, but I didn't have a chance against Max. He grabbed me in a headlock, ripped my bag from my grip and threw me into the room, slamming the door behind me and turning the key.

After a few seconds I forced myself to calm down, knowing that was my only chance of finding a way out. I looked around the room. There was a double bed, made up with fairly clean bedclothes. In fact it looked pretty much like a normal bedroom apart from the fact that the window had been boarded up with screws, cutting out all natural light and the only chance of escape. There was a flimsy wardrobe, which let a stale smell out into the room when I opened the doors. My fear was making me angry and I went back to the door, kicking and banging and shouting to be let out. After a minute I heard footsteps outside. The key clicked in the lock and the door flew open as Max burst in and punched me hard in the side of the head, knocking me to the floor with an explosion of light in my brain.

'Bang this door again,' he shouted, 'and I will seriously hurt you.'

I was crying like a baby. I was mainly angry with myself for letting my guard down and allowing myself to fall into a trap that I should have seen coming. I felt so stupid and so frightened.

'Listen,' he said, softening his tone a little. 'If you just show me some respect and do what I tell you, we are going to get on fine.'

He left the room again, locking the door after him, leaving me to think about what he had said and to ponder on the idea that he deserved my respect just because he was stronger than me and because I was in his house.

A few minutes later the door opened again and Jake came in. I could see Max hovering behind him, so I knew it was his idea for Jake to talk to me.

'I want to get out of here, Jake,' I said.

'He won't let you go.'

'You fucking bastard.'

'I didn't know he was going to do this to you,' he lied. 'Look, just do what they want you to do. You'll get paid and you won't get hurt. It's an easy way to get money.'

'I don't want to do it, Jake! I want to get out. They're keeping me a prisoner.'

'You have to do it – otherwise he is going to hurt you. Listen, he's all right, this guy who's coming. He's a decent bloke. He's a bit rough, but if you do what you're told it shouldn't be a problem.'

Realizing that he wasn't getting anywhere with me, Jake went back to the door and tapped some pre-arranged signal. Max opened the door from the outside and I tried to go out with Jake.

'Back,' Max snarled and I could see he was going to hit me again if I disobeyed. The door shut behind Jake and the lock clicked again.

Max was back a few minutes later. 'Just remember,' he said, 'respect. Respect – otherwise you are going to have me to deal with.'

The punter came in and Max introduced us and then left the room with a cheery 'Enjoy yourselves', locking us in as he went.

The guy looked about fifty years old to me, well groomed and dressed like any normal man from the street. He sat on the bed, patting a place next to him.

'Come and sit with me,' he said.

'I don't want to.'

'I'm not going to hurt you. Just come and talk to me.'

I wondered if I might be able to talk him out of whatever he was planning to do to me, so I sat down gingerly beside him. He patted my knee.

'We'll just play around,' he said.

'I don't want to do anything with you,' I said. 'I'm not like that.'

'That's not what Jake told me. He said you like all that stuff.'

I remembered how I had told Jake about things that had happened to me in the past. He must have told this guy that I'd had this sort of thing happen to me before, so I would know the score. He must have told Max all about it, and now they had told this guy. They thought because I had been groomed as a child it would just be a matter of easing me back into it. I couldn't stop the tears from running down my cheeks as he started kissing me quite forcefully.

'Just do what I tell you,' he murmured into my ear, 'and then I'll be gone. You know you want this really.'

His breath stank of whatever he had eaten that day as he tried to kiss me on the mouth and I instinctively pushed him away. His hands were attempting to pull down my trousers as I tried to wriggle away from his powerful grip. There was a rap on the door and I heard Max's voice on the other side.

'Everything OK in there?'

'No,' the punter shouted back. 'He's playing me up.'

The door opened and Max came in with Brad right behind him. The punter jumped off me, his zip undone and his shirt hanging out, watching as the two of them gave me a real hiding on the bed, punching me in the stomach over and over again, throwing me around like a rag doll. They stripped me naked and then threw me back on the bed, leaving me gasping for breath and unable to move. All through the beating the punter was cheering them on, encouraging them to teach me a lesson I wouldn't forget. Inside my head I had flashes of the time when Amani, my mum's boyfriend, had first brought Uncle Douglas into a room with me. I was only nine years old then and weak with hunger and lack of exercise, but I'd still resisted Uncle Douglas's advances. And Amani had beaten me in just the same way as Max and Brad were now doing. Was I never going to escape from these people? Was this sort of thing going to go on happening to me until someone eventually killed me or until I was so battered no one wanted to have anything to do with me any more?

My ribs felt as if they were broken and I could sense an asthma attack coming on as I battled to get some air into my lungs, to at least stay alive through the ordeal. When they were sure they had broken down any signs of resistance in me, Max and Brad went out and left the punter to do what he wanted. I could hardly breathe, and I didn't have enough strength left to fight both the pain and the man. As I struggled for air, he rolled me on to my front and raped me. He had become so excited during the beating that it was all over in minutes and he dressed and left the room as if nothing unusual had happened. I could hear their voices talking about me outside.

'This one is a good one,' the punter was saying.

I lay still, shaking and crying from the shock, praying that the pain would pass, calling for Dad to get me out of that flat, not knowing whether Max was going to let me go now or whether I was doomed to stay locked in the room for days or weeks or months. About ten minutes later Max came back in, having seen his customer out of the flat, I guess.

'You little bastard,' he shouted. 'I told you "respect", didn't I?'

He pulled his trousers down, pushed me hard down on to the bed and raped me too, a hundred times more violently than the punter had. I could tell he was doing it to teach me a lesson, to make sure that I never forgot what would happen to me if I ever disobeyed him again.

The pain was so great that I was unable to stop myself from vomiting on the floor beside the bed as he climbed off me.

'You dirty little bastard,' he said contemptuously, banging on the door for Brad to let him out. I crawled into the corner of the room, still being sick as I struggled back into my clothes, terrified of what was going to happen next, feeling filthy and defiled.

Eventually Jake came back in.

'Look what they've done to me, Jake,' I said.

'I know. Why didn't you just do what the guy wanted, like I told you? Max is only being nasty to you because you're not doing what you're told. You won't get paid for this now because you played up.'

'Please get me out.'

'I can't. You're going to have to be reasonable now and win Max over. I'll have a word with him and try to get you out tonight. Just promise me you're going to behave yourself.'

'Yeah,' I said, knowing now there was no point in fighting any more. 'Tell Max I'm really sorry.'

He'd been told to clear up where I'd thrown up and then to leave me alone. Time passed as I waited for Max to cool down. I knew that my only chance of escaping with my life was to keep quiet and look as if they had broken my spirit. Once I was back on the outside I could think what to do about never letting myself get into a position like this again. Jake brought me some food and water, but I couldn't face eating anything. A few hours later Brad came up to fetch me and I limped out behind him in a daze, terrified that I was going to get another beating.

The first thing I saw in the lounge was Max going through my bag. He looked up as I came in and waved Mohamed's money at me.

'Where did you get this, boy?'

'You can have it. It was given to me when I come down.'

'I don't want your money, boy, as long as you behave and do what you're told next time.'

'Yeah, Max. I'm really sorry about that. I'll do whatever you say next time.'

My only thought was to get out of the flat and away from Max. I would have said anything at that stage.

'That's what I wanted to hear,' he said, grinning, shoving my money back into the bag. Reaching into his pocket he pulled out a fiver. 'And that's for earlier.' He put it into the bag too and tossed it across to me. I was shaking so much I almost dropped it.

'Cool down, man,' he said. 'I'm sorry for what I had to do to you, but you've got to understand, respect is what is needed. You work for me now. I'm your boss now.'

He gestured for me to sit down, as if I should be relaxing, but I couldn't stop myself from flinching every time he walked past me, expecting to receive another smack. I was trying to decide what to do. Should I make a run for it? But I could hardly even walk, so they would easily catch me and then they would probably throw me over the balcony, or drag me back in and give me another beating. He brought me a glass of cider and told me to drink. My hand was shaking so much I couldn't manage it, so he lifted it to my lips as if I was a baby. It tasted disgusting, but it dulled the pain a bit.

'That's my boy!' he cheered as I drained it. He got me another and kept them coming until I eventually fell into a drunken sleep. It was as if I had passed some sort of test and now I could be one of them, getting drunk with them, passing out on the sofa with them.

Chapter Nine

The Great Escape

When I woke up I felt as if I'd been hit by a truck.

'Come on, boy,' Max said as he came into the room in his boxers and vest and saw me stirring. 'Got a hangover, have you?'

'Got a headache,' I mumbled, flinching away from him.

'Here. Take these.' He gave me some pills, as if we were best mates and he was just helping me out, looking after me.

He was acting as if nothing unusual had happened, as if life in the flat was just going on as normal. Nobody said anything about me going and I didn't dare to raise the subject for fear of angering him. I was just going to have to wait and see what happened.

'We're going out tonight,' he told me halfway through the afternoon. 'We've got a party to go to. One of my punters has asked me to bring a few boys to his place.'

I tried to sound as if that was a great idea, but I felt sick at the thought of why Max's punters would want him to bring boys like me and Jake along. If there were a whole bunch of them, things could get really violent and unpleasant, as they used to on the weekends when I was kept at Uncle Douglas's house. How was I going to get a chance to escape between now and then without getting another beating?

The afternoon dragged past as I tried to look as if I was relaxed and willingly fitting in with Max's plans. Finally we left to go to the party. I was still having difficulty walking after the beating I had received the night before, and I felt sick with anxiety about what lay in store for me at our destination. As we walked out to the car, Jake said he had to stop by the Strand on the way to pick something up. Max was really pissed off at having his plans interrupted and tried to talk him out of it as we drove across London, but Jake insisted it would just take a minute. I guess Max still didn't trust me not to try to do a runner and let him down with the punters he'd lined up for the night.

'All right,' he said eventually, gesturing towards me, 'but he's staying with me in the car.'

Before getting to the Strand we drew up at a street corner somewhere and another young lad jumped into the back of the car with me and Jake, squashing me in the middle. They all seemed to know him. He was sporting a black eye but looked more relaxed and accepting of the whole thing than I felt. I realized that Max must be running a whole string of rent boys and that he now considered me to be part of the business. Brad, the minder, was sitting in the front passenger seat beside Max. All my worst fears about being trapped in the back of a car were rising to the top of my brain. I was close to screaming but I held it together, knowing what would happen to me if I made any sort of fuss at all.

We reached the Strand and pulled over beside the kerb, as I had seen Max do before.

'I won't be a second,' Jake said, and reached for the door lock. For some reason he was clutching my bag and I was frightened he was making off with my money now he knew it was there.

'That's my stuff,' I protested.

'You fucking stay there,' Max snapped, swivelling in his seat and glowering at me.

As the car door opened, I spotted Jock hovering a few yards away in a shop doorway and made an instant decision. Barging past Jake, I started shouting.

'Jock! Jock! Jock! Help me.'

Max and Brad were both out of the car within seconds as a puzzled-looking Jock lurched forward to see what all the fuss was about. Max tried to grab me, and even through the haze of drink that was obviously fogging his brain Jock instantly worked out what was going on, coming to my defence with a stream of swear words which brought others running across the street to back him up. Anyone who lives on the street likes a distraction from the boredom of the endless days and nights.

'They've hurt me, Jock,' I screamed. 'They've hurt me.'

It all became confusing and noisy. There were fists and boots flying in every direction. Jock's girlfriend, Charlotte, grabbed my hand in the middle of the turmoil and started to run, dragging me behind her. Jake must have decided he would be in trouble with Max and Brad too, because he came running after us. Maybe he didn't want Jock to think he was siding with Max. As he came close, I lashed out at him in order to grab my bag, accidentally hitting him in the face with my elbow and sending him flying to the floor. My overriding instinct was to get away from Max and Brad, but I didn't trust Jake either.

I was shaking with fear and gasping for breath, desperate to get clear of the lit street and to find somewhere to hide. Charlotte ducked down a side road, still holding on to my hand, and led me round to the back of the outreach centre, which was closed because it was a Sunday. There was a small fenced garden there with some bushes that we could hide in. She hustled me deep into the shrubbery and we both sat very still, listening for footsteps and shouting, and struggling to get our breath back.

'What's going on?' I whispered after a few minutes of silence.

'I'll go and find out,' she whispered back. 'You stay here.'

'No, don't leave me.' I grabbed her arm and hung on. I didn't want to be left on my own. She must have seen how frightened I was because she gave me a little cuddle, which felt nice but didn't help the fear.

'It's all right,' she cooed. 'You're going to be all right.'

'They're gonna kill me,' I kept saying, over and over again. 'They're gonna hurt me again.'

'No, you're safe now. Jock won't let anything happen to you. We've been looking everywhere for you. Where have you been?'

I didn't answer because I was too embarrassed to admit that I had got into a car with Max after all the warnings I had been given, and I felt ashamed of the things that I had let them do to me. Charlotte didn't push it; she probably knew enough to be able to guess most of it. About half an hour later there was a rustling in the bushes.

'They're coming to get me,' I hissed, clinging even more tightly on to Charlotte's arm, shaking and terrified for my life.

'Shh,' she said, trying to calm me. 'No one knows about this place except us.'

The bushes parted and Jock appeared beside us, hauling Jake along with him by the scruff of his scrawny little neck. I didn't want anything to do with Jake. I felt he had betrayed me and I believed he would do it again if he had a chance. Jock must have worked out exactly what had happened, because he threw Jake down on the ground and started laying into him, despite the fact that he was obviously pretty drunk. The rest of Jock's gang were now weaving their way into the garden, asking me how I was, assuring me they would look after me now and cursing Max and Jake.

'Now you give him a kicking,' Jock told me, standing back from Jake, who was lying on the ground, curled up in a foetal position with his arms up to protect his head and face. As the fear in me subsided, the anger at what I had been put through at Max's flat and how Jake had led me into it when he knew exactly what lay in store for me bubbled up to the surface and I laid into him in a blind rage. Jake stayed on the ground, curled up in a ball, knowing he had no choice but to take his punishment. I was sorry that doling it out didn't make me feel any better.

It was getting late by then and the others were thinking about going in search of cardboard boxes and heading down to the park, where people would already be starting to construct their shelters for the night, laying claim to the best sites.

'I don't want to go out there,' I told Jock. 'Max is still going to be looking for me and I don't want to be in a box on my own in the open, where he can just pull me out in the middle of the night when everyone else is asleep. I want to stay here, where I can't be seen. And I ain't going to no soup kitchen where anyone might spot me.'

Jock was trying to focus his fuzzy brain on what I was saying, nodding sagely all the time, his eyes rolling about the place. I could see there was a limit to how far I could rely on him to look after me.

'All right,' he slurred eventually. 'Charlotte and a couple of the boys will stay here with you and the rest of us will go and find you some food and boxes. Then we'll set up here for the night.'

The guys he left with me were as drunk and falling over as he was and probably wouldn't have been much use if Max and Brad had turned up, but at least I wasn't alone, and at least I was tucked away in a place where there were no casual passers-by.

'I'll have to leave London tomorrow,' I told Charlotte as we waited. 'Otherwise I'm going to be bumping into Max all the time and sooner or later he's going to find a way to get me on my own without Jock around to protect me.'

'There's other places in London apart from Charing Cross,' she assured me. 'We'll find you somewhere to go in the morning.'

I kept on insisting, because at that moment I wanted to be as far from London as I could possibly manage. I wished I knew of some other place to go that would be better.

By the time Jock got back with the cardboard and food I had managed to convince Charlotte that leaving the city would be for the best and she stuck up for me when Jock tried to dissuade me. When morning broke and we knew the centre would be open, I was still scared at the thought of leaving the safety of the bushes, even for the short walk round the corner in broad daylight.

'What if Max is waiting there?' I asked, shivering at the thought. 'He knows that's where we all go.'

'He wouldn't come there,' Josh assured me. 'He understands they'd kick him out. Everyone knows about him and what he's about.'

Charlotte had already been in there ahead of us by the time Jock and I arrived and had told a Jamaican volunteer what had happened to me.

'Let me talk to him,' the guy had said.

The only black guy I had ever really known at that stage was Amani, the man who had been my uncle first, then moved in with my mother and become my main torturer and most regular rapist during my years imprisoned in the cellar. He and Mum had later sold me to punters in exactly the same way Max had. Having had no education in geography or history or anything else, I had no idea about where different people of different races came from; all I knew was that everything about this Jamaican guy brought back terrible memories of the things that Amani had done to me over the years, which was why I had been steering clear of him up till then. It was a purely instinctive animal fear that coursed through me when he came over to talk to me that day.

83

'I've heard what's happened to you,' he said in what I now realize was a kind voice.

'Fuck off and leave me alone,' I shouted, immediately afraid and defensive.

'What are you being like that for?' he asked, looking genuinely taken aback. 'I'm just offering to talk to you.'

'I want to speak to a white person,' I yelled, having no idea that what I was saying was deeply offensive and quite probably illegal.

Incensed by my ignorant attack, he forgot all his training and launched himself at me. Filled with panic and fear and anger, seeing only Amani's face in my mind's eye and desperate to escape a beating, I grabbed a paperweight off the desk and hit him hard on the head with it. It must have been a powerful blow because it brought him to his knees, even though he was a big guy. As he shook his head and tried to pull himself back on to his feet, I made a run for it, clutching my bag as always, barging past Jock in my haste to make a getaway.

'Oh my fuck,' Jock said. 'What's he done to him?'

He, Jake and Charlotte ran after me and eventually caught up with me in the street, hauling me round a corner and out of sight.

'They'll be calling the police to you after that,' Charlotte said once she got her breath. I could hear sirens going and immediately feared they were coming for me. Had I killed the man?

'We've got to get him out of London now,' Jock said, apparently sobered by the sudden burst of activity and excitement.

Jake seemed to be keen to get away from London and Max as well. He knew that he was going to be in for a beating himself for what had happened the previous evening, as it had been because of him we had pulled up in the Strand, giving me my chance to escape. Although I still didn't trust Jake, I felt that it was up to Jock and Charlotte whether they let him come. They seemed to think he was part of their gang, so we all walked to the mainline station. My eyes were darting in every direction at once; I was certain I would hear a screech of tyres at any second and find myself thrown on to the back seat of a speeding Mercedes.

'I know where it would be best to go,' Jock said, pointing at the departures board.

'Yeah,' Charlotte agreed. 'We know a lot of people there, Joe. You'll be safe there.'

'Plenty of homeless people there,' Jock went on. 'I was there before I came to Charing Cross. I go back and forth to a squat there sometimes. Max wouldn't know about it.'

Once we were on the train, I immediately felt safer. We were all being pretty loud, the others still being drunk from the night before and now high on the excitement of our morning's activities, and we were all shouting and swearing a fair bit to keep our courage up. It felt good to be part of such a close group, even if one of them was Jake, and I wanted the rest of the passengers on the train to see that I wasn't a sad loner any more, that I was part of a gang and that I wasn't going to allow myself to be a victim any longer.

Chapter Ten

The Squat

'I don't know for sure if I'll be able to get you in here,' Jock admitted as we lurched off the train at our destination and headed for the squat.

By this stage the idea of living in a community had taken on the same romantic appeal for me as Charing Cross had when I was stranded on the side of the motorway slip road. I could hardly imagine how great it would be to be living with my friends in a warm, dry house of our own, surrounded by like-minded people. I believed I would feel like a king in his own castle.

'Even though they know me, they can be a bit funny about new people,' Jock went on, preparing me for the worst. 'There aren't that many squats around here, so people tend to want to keep them to themselves, if you know what I mean.'

He led us through a few quite nice streets and finally came to a halt in front of a big old house which had all its windows boarded up. It looked as if it had once been an office of some sort, maybe for a dentist or a doctor or someone like that, with accommodation or flats upstairs. There was a big gravel car park in front of the house but no cars. It looked desolate and a little forbidding from the outside.

As we crunched across the gravel, I felt my nerves building up again. I didn't like the look of the boarded windows. They reminded me too much of being trapped in the cellar, or in Uncle Doug's vile house, or in the bedroom of Max's flat. I hated the idea of not being able to easily escape from any place if things turned nasty – which in my experience they always did in the end. I didn't like the idea of being trapped anywhere, because that was when things always went worst for me. The great thing about being out on the streets had been the feeling that I could run away at any moment if danger threatened. I had no idea what was going on inside this lifeless-looking building and by the time I found out it would be too late to make a run for freedom. At the same time I did like the idea of being safe and warm indoors.

My instinct was always to distrust everyone until they proved they were sound, but I knew at some stage I had to put my faith in someone if I didn't want to live like a frightened animal all my life, and if I wanted to be a permanent member of any group of people. Jock had always stuck up for me whenever he was around and conscious, so I had to believe that he wouldn't take me somewhere that was dangerous, especially with Charlotte there as well. I might not be able to trust Jake, but I felt I had to trust the other two because they had earned it. Jock had actually physically fought for me on the street the previous night and now he was bringing me to a safe place, using up favours from other people. So few people in my life had ever stuck up for me or tried to help me since Dad had died that it was hard to know how to react to someone who did. Even my brother Wally, who had tried to be kind to me during my imprisonment in the cellar, had never actually done anything about sending help once he was free of the house himself. What Jock and Charlotte were doing for me meant a lot to me.

We went round the house to a side entrance and Jock banged on the door with some sort of pre-arranged code. A few seconds later the door opened a crack and a pair of eyes appeared on the other side.

'Jock!' The eyes turned into the house and shouted out the news. 'It's Jock!'

The door opened immediately and we were swept inside amidst a bunch of new faces. Just as on the streets of London, everyone in the house seemed to know Jock and to be pleased to see him.

'Come in, Jock.'

'Charlotte's here too,' Jock said. 'And I've got some mates with me.'

I could hear girls' voices asking one another what was going on, passing on the news that it was Jock, sounding pleased. As my eyes adjusted to the room, I saw them all rushing up to give Jock a cuddle and I noticed Charlotte getting a bit stony-faced. She needn't have worried, because most of them were really rough. Once we were inside and I realized there was no threat to my safety, it seemed a very comfortable house. It was quite clean, despite the fact that people's clothes were strewn over every surface, and really warm, because for some reason the electricity was still working and there was central heating.

There seemed to be dozens of people and it was a while before I was able to sort them out and work out that there were actually about fifteen of them living in the house. The boys were less effusive than the girls in their welcome, circling Jake and me warily, obviously wondering who we were and whether we posed any sort of threat.

'I hope they're not staying here, Jock,' one of them said when he didn't think I was listening.

'Come on,' Jock said, grinning and slapping him on the back. 'Give them a break.'

'He'll never let two of them in,' the other man said.

I discovered that the man they were talking about was called Ben. He was head of the squat, but he was out of the house when we arrived. I felt quite intimidated at the thought that there might be an authority figure who could give the thumbs up or down to us being allowed to stay. I kept quiet as the others all introduced themselves.

'Don't he fucking talk, Jock?' one of the girls asked.

'He's just a kid,' Jock said and I wished I could think of something to say that would show I wasn't.

Ben arrived back with a girl and seemed as pleased to see Jock as everyone else had been. 'Jocky, boy! Where have you fucking been? You haven't been down here for months.'

'I need you to do me a favour, Ben,' Jock said once the greetings were over. 'I need you to take two lads in for me.'

'Listen, mate, there's no room here. The rooms are all taken.'

'They can sleep on the floor – they're not bothered.'

The two of them went outside to chat about it and at that moment a girl came into the room who didn't look like any of the others. She looked clean and well groomed, with her wavy hair pulled up into a tight bun which showed off her face. I thought she was the prettiest girl I had ever seen. The moment she walked into the room she stared at me and then smiled in a way that made my insides feel like water.

'What's your name then?' she asked.

'Joe,' I stuttered.

'Hi,' she smiled again, staring straight into my eyes. 'I'm Lisa.'

Jake gave me a nudge in the ribs. 'I think she likes you.'

'Fuck off, Jake,' I said, giving him a shove and feeling the blood rushing to my face as the girl continued to stare at me.

I don't know what Jock had said to Ben, but when they came back into the room he said that Jake and I could stay.

'Oh, I know he's staying,' Lisa said, nodding towards me. 'He's cute. He's my blue-eyed boy.'

The more little comments she made about me the more annoyed I could see the other boys becoming, the darker I blushed and the more incapable I became of speaking. Now Lisa had drawn their attention to me, the other girls were starting to show an interest too.

'Eyes off!' Lisa snapped and I noticed how quickly they obeyed, as if they were frightened of her, as if she was the boss.

That afternoon the others showed me around the area, taking me to the outreach centre, which was housed in a few conjoined Portakabins a couple of streets away. The volunteers there seemed to be more organized than those in London. There was a black guy working there called Tom, but by then Jock had explained to me why it was wrong to say anything or judge anyone by the colour of their skin. It was as if Jock was educating me in some of the social skills I had missed out on in the years when I had been kept prisoner. Now that I was thinking more clearly, I realized that this guy was really nice and nothing like Amani, and I could understand

92

now why the Jamaican in London had taken such exception to my attitude. Tom spent a lot of time with me and taught me a lot more about the history of slavery and Africa and racism. In the end I got to trust him so much that I was able to confess what I had done to the Jamaican volunteer in London.

'Well, that's a shame,' he said, 'but I'm not going to tell anyone. I don't think you'll be doing anything like that again, will you?'

I promised solemnly that I wouldn't.

Whenever new people arrived in the area the staff at the centre encouraged them to have a check-up with the doctor. I had found the doctor in London really helpful about my asthma, so I was happy to do that. The first thing he did once he had written down my details was to take a blood sample to test for HIV.

'I'm not saying you've got anything,' he said, 'and I don't want to worry you, but it is a standard procedure.'

'What's HIV?' I asked, showing yet another massive gap in my knowledge of the world around me. I guess other children soak up these sorts of facts by socializing and listening to adults as well as by going to school. By keeping me in the cellar all that time, Mum had put me about three years behind where I should have been when it came to general knowledge and an understanding of things in general. When the doctor explained what it was and how it could be spread, I started to shake with fear again. When I thought back to all the men who had raped me as a child without using any protection, not to mention Max and his punter, it seemed I was about as high risk as it was possible to be without being a junkie sharing other people's needles. Every act that he mentioned as being high risk I remembered having had done to me at some stage, and the panic grew until I was unable to hide how agitated I was.

'How long will these tests take to come back?' I asked.

'A month,' he replied.

'A month?'

I thought I was going to pass out. How was I going to be able to live with this anxiety for that long? I was now convinced that I was going to die of HIV before I had even had a chance to find the love of my life.

The doctor was a kind man and must have been able to see how hysterical I was, and he promised to get my test done as a priority.

'I'll let them know at the centre when I have the results and you need to come in and see me again,' he said.

I went back to the squat with my nerves jangling, to find Lisa eagerly awaiting my return.

Chapter Eleven

Lisa

Lisa was waiting to take up where she left off with her flirting and teasing, which was throwing me into a bit of a panic. It wasn't that I didn't fancy her, because I did; I just didn't know what to say to her or how to react to the way she was coming on to me. I had no experience upon which to draw, because no one had ever teased me like this before, and I had never felt attracted to anyone in this way before either.

She was actually less than two years older than me, but she was a hundred times more confident and worldly. I could see that all the other boys in the house fancied her and tried to impress her or catch her attention, but she just brushed them off and concentrated all her attentions on me. Her interest in me obviously mystified the others as much as it mystified me. I was such a scrawny-looking dork with a ridiculous pudding-basin haircut – how could anyone fancy me?

Even Charlotte was surprised by the way Lisa was coming on to me.

'It's not like her,' she laughed. 'She doesn't usually give any of the boys a chance, but she really seems to like you.'

As the evening wore on, Lisa separated me from the others, telling Jake to piss off when he didn't take the hint quickly enough for her liking. She sat down beside me and we started talking properly in a way I had never talked to any girl before. Like the homeless kids I'd met in London, she'd had an awful childhood, constantly being raped by her dad from the age of four until finally she ran away from home. When she eventually spoke up about what was happening to her, her mother turned on her, telling her what a dirty little slag she was, as if it was all her fault. Her parents' marriage collapsed soon after that, but it was too late for Lisa to be able to rebuild her relationship with her mother. Her experiences had made her very reluctant to sleep around like the other girls in the house. I could understand her reluctance to get physically close to anyone else completely: like me, she had only ever known it to end in violence and pain.

'These others are fucking slags,' she told me contemptuously. 'They'll sleep with anything in here. Stay away from them. They've all got sexually transmitted diseases too. You'll catch the lot if you go anywhere near them.'

The girls must have known how she felt about them and seemed to steer clear of her, as if wary of upsetting her. She got on better with the lads and would happily hang around with them as long as they didn't try to touch her. The only girl she had any time for was Charlotte.

'Charlotte has told me a bit about what you went through,' she said.

By that time I had already realized that Charlotte was the biggest gossip going, but somehow I didn't mind that Lisa knew such private things about me, especially if it had made her feel able to open up about her own past. I felt safe with her, protected. When she found out what had happened to me in London she laid into Jake so hard I actually started to feel quite sorry for the poor lad. It seemed as if he ended up being everyone's punch bag. Actually I didn't think he was that bad – just weak and lacking in any moral courage. Lisa said I was being too soft on him. Once she knew, she wanted him to leave the squat, and every time she saw him she couldn't resist giving him another slap. But he still stayed around, dodging the punches, which confirmed my suspicion that he didn't have much personal pride.

Jake had managed to pal up with one of the other boys that first evening in the house and the guy said Jake could share his room. But no one offered me a place, which I found a bit hurtful. I couldn't understand how Jake had got an offer straight away and I hadn't. It was only much later that I discovered they had all been warned off suggesting I share with them.

'I might have to sleep outside tonight,' I told Lisa as it grew late and the others started peeling off to their beds.

'Oh?' she said innocently. 'Why's that then?'

'None of the others want me in their rooms.'

'You'll have to share my room then,' she said. 'It's only small but we'll be OK.'

Small was hardly the word for it. It was pretty much a box room, the floor completely covered with a double mattress and a pile of her abandoned clothes.

'Are you sure?' I asked doubtfully, looking around for a corner that I could curl up in, alarms going off somewhere deep inside my head. I was happy that she was willing to be my friend like this, but not sure what was expected in return.

'Yeah,' she said. 'I don't mind, as long as you don't try anything on.'

She didn't have to worry about that. I had seen how hard she could hit, so I wasn't planning to do anything that might incur her anger. Despite my reservations, I was grateful to her for the offer and tired enough to take it up without any further argument. I kept my clothes on and climbed into my own grubby sleeping bag, which I had brought down with me from London. Lisa didn't undress either. She was wearing a long kaftan and a pair of socks and had a double sleeping bag that she wrapped herself up in beside me.

'You go by the wall,' Lisa said, 'because I don't like being closed in.'

Nor do I, I thought, but I didn't dare say anything since she was giving up half her bed and I didn't want to seem ungrateful or to have to go out into the cold now I was so cosy. Although I knew she had been teasing me and pretending to fancy me, I had never felt so safe and secure with anyone before in my life. There was a warm glow inside me like I sometimes used to get when I thought about my dad and how he used to be with me. I guess it was love, but I didn't know it at the time; I just knew it felt really nice.

I had turned to face the wall and was about to drop off to sleep after a long and eventful day when I felt something tickling the back of my hair. Thinking it might be a spider, I went to brush it away and found Lisa's fingers there. She didn't make any attempt to move them away, coming closer instead and kissing the back of my neck. I froze, not sure what to do. I wanted to turn round and kiss her back, but I was frightened of doing it wrong and getting hit as Jake had got hit earlier. Terrified of misreading the signals, I decided to stay very still and pretend I was asleep. She moved a few inches closer and started nibbling my ear.

'Are you asleep?' she whispered.

I scrunched my eyes as tightly shut as I could manage.

'I know you're awake,' she said, and she started tickling me and making me laugh.

'I'm asleep,' I protested.

'Oh, are you?' she said, laughing.

'You woke me up.'

'I've got a little problem,' she said. 'I'm really cold in this sleeping bag. Why don't you come in and keep me warm?'

'Can I put my sleeping bag in yours?'

'No, that won't work. I need you to cuddle up to me to warm me up. Before you get in, take that shell suit off because it's not very nice material, is it?'

'Can I keep my trousers on?'

'No, take them off. You'll get really hot in here.'

Unbelievable though it seems as I write these words now, I genuinely thought in my innocence that because everyone had told me how she didn't sleep around, she actually wouldn't try anything on if I did as she asked. I completely believed that she just wanted me to get into her sleeping bag in order to keep her warm.

Once I had done everything she instructed, we lay together, scrunched up close, me with my back to her again and her with her arms round me. It felt like the best place in the world to be. When her hands started to roam down my body, I was genuinely shocked but excited at the same time. She started trying to turn me around to face her and I tried to resist. I didn't want her to think that I was jumping on her at the first opportunity. I still thought she might be testing me and I was determined to prove that I was no slag either.

I held out for about half an hour and then we made love. It was the most beautiful experience I had ever had, even though it was quite physically painful because of my lack of technique and experience. I was used to being raped and abused, not to being loved and encouraged to take the lead. By the end I was crying, partly from the pain but mainly from the emotion of having someone treat me like a person for the first time rather than a lump of meat. Lisa was so sweet and understanding and kind that I was deeply in love from that night onwards. I felt I had met the person I had come south to search for.

The first thought that came into my head when I woke up the next morning with Lisa in my arms was that I had given her HIV. In the excitement and confusion of the previous night I had completely forgotten that I was waiting for my test results and only a few hours before had been worried sick that I was infected. A terrible sense of dread took hold of my heart.

She could see something was worrying me and asked what was wrong. When I told her she just laughed, as if I was being silly.

'Oh, you'll be all right,' she dismissed my fears. 'Everyone has to do those tests and I've never known anyone be positive.'

Her confidence made me feel a bit better for a few minutes, but once I was out of the warmth of the sleeping bag my doubts and fears soon crept back into my head. I was still convinced that it was going to be bad news and when I got a message at the centre four days later telling me to go and see the doctor urgently I felt sick with fear and certain he was going to tell me I was dying. I went straight round with Jock, leaving him in the waiting room as I went in.

'Sit down, Joe,' the doctor said, getting out my notes. I forced myself to sit and stay silent when I actually wanted to scream at him.

'Have I got it? Have I got it?'

'Panic over,' he smiled. 'Your tests have come back clean. It's very unlikely you have anything, but there is an incubation period, so we will need to test you again in a few weeks.'

'Oh, thanks, doc.'

I'd stopped listening by that stage, my thoughts overwhelmed with a mixture of joy and relief. I had been terrified to let Lisa even touch me after the first night in case I was positive, certain in my mind that I would soon be wasting away with full-blown AIDS. Suddenly the weight of the whole world seemed to be lifted from my shoulders. Life seemed so sweet as I danced out of the surgery through the waiting room full of people, shouting out loud to Jock and the whole world.

'I don't have HIV! I don't have HIV!'

I could see looks of apprehension passing over the faces of some of the women. I must have looked like a madman, but I just couldn't hold in my joy. I couldn't wait to get back to Lisa at the house to tell her that I was all clear and to repeat the joys of our first night together.

In the following weeks she continued to make it very clear to everyone that I was her property and the rest of them had to keep their hands off, which made me feel loved and secure and cared about for the first time in my life. It was the most wonderful feeling to wake up each morning next to her, knowing that I wasn't alone in the world any more. My only complaint was that she was very bossy, always telling me what to do all the time. Having been controlled by other people all my life, I found it hard to take orders from anyone, particularly a woman, without feeling the same fears and resentments and hatreds that I had suppressed for so many years when I had been beaten into subservience. There were moments when I would feel a glimmer of the anger I used to feel for Mum when she forced me to do whatever she wanted, but then Lisa would do or say something so sweet to me that my anger would melt away again as quickly as it had risen. I knew that the problem was mine and not hers, and I struggled to control my temper and my instinct to fight back and argue every time she told me to do something. I never wanted to do anything that might endanger our love for even a second.

It was as if I had found my soulmate, which was an amazing feeling for someone who had always felt isolated and threatened by everyone around him. She was the first person to love me since my dad had died more than ten years earlier.

The others used to go out during the day, begging on the streets, but Lisa and I didn't want to do that. We believed we had all we needed in the way of food and extra clothes from the centre, and the house was perfectly warm and comfortable, so we didn't need money badly enough to demean ourselves by asking for more charity.

The other lads in the house were always giving Lisa a share of their money anyway because they liked her, so she was never short of cash to use to buy the drink that she liked. I had thought Jock was a big drinker, but Lisa was worse than him, and always on hard stuff like vodka. She didn't seem to be able to function at all without a few shots inside her. Because we spent all our time together it wasn't long before I had a regular habit too, both drinking and smoking. It's hard to live amongst people twenty-four hours a day and not start to behave like them. As a result I was constantly getting headaches and then taking another drink to try to get rid of them. Everyone in the house was pretty much the same, so there was no one to explain to me that the more I drank the worse I was making things for myself.

Despite the quantities that she drank, Lisa never seemed to be drunk like Jock, though, falling about the place or slurring her words; she would just be constantly pouring herself another shot. I guess it was her way of dealing with the pain she was carrying around inside her head from the things her dad had done to her. I could completely understand that. She self-harmed as well, slashing at her wrists – a habit I wouldn't pick up till later. When I first saw her doing it, I couldn't see why she felt the need and asked why she did it.

'It's like a release,' she explained. 'Like relieving all the tension that builds up inside my head.'

As I say, it was as if we were soulmates.

Chapter Twelve

Street Crime

There was no question that Ben was the boss of the house, and he made it clear that if Jake and I wanted to stay there we had to pull our weight and that we couldn't just sit around the house all day enjoying ourselves, even though he was happy for Lisa to do whatever she wanted. I'd noticed that everyone let Lisa do what she wanted.

'If you're staying in my squat,' he told us, 'you have to work for me.'

Jock and Charlotte were already earning their keep by doing a bit of thieving for him and he told us we had to do the same. Lisa wasn't happy at the idea of me being involved in anything like that, but she seemed to think I didn't really have a choice if I was going to stay.

Ben was a broad cockney guy who was a lot more grown up and organized than the rest of us. I went into his room once and it was like a normal bedroom in a normal house, full of nice things and done up nicely. It was nothing like the other rooms in the squat. Because it was at the back of the house he had even taken the boards off the window, so he had curtains and natural light while the rest of us lived like moles. I thought perhaps if I could make a bit of money like him, maybe Lisa and I could do our room up as well and improve our lives as Ben had. I was already thinking as if I was part of a permanent couple, making plans and dreaming dreams of better things to come.

Ben's clothes were a lot smarter than anything the rest of us had too, all expensive brand names, which he had bought from proper shops and kept all the receipts for. If we had ever been raided, the police would never have found any stolen goods on Ben or in his room: he was much too canny for that.

'I'm coming too,' Lisa announced to the others the first night I was due to go out with them. 'I'm watching over him. I don't trust you lot to look after him.'

'You don't have to be attached to him every second of the day, do you?' Ben protested.

'I'm going to watch out for him. All right?'

'No.' Ben said. It was unusual to see anyone stand up to Lisa, even Ben. 'You stay here.'

Then Charlotte said she wanted to come to be with Jock, but Ben wasn't having that either.

'You stay here and keep Lisa company,' he instructed and they both subsided, grumbling.

As we lived inside a house with boarded windows, our days and nights all merged into one. We lived to a different schedule to that of the outside world, often sleeping through the mornings and coming alive in the evenings. So it was well past midnight by the time Ben, Jock, Jake and I sauntered out into the deserted town centre. My stomach was churning as we strolled around, like little kings of all we surveyed. I tried to look as if I was as confident as the others, but I was actually feeling horribly exposed and vulnerable, just wanting to be safely back in the warmth of the house, behind boarded windows with Lisa.

Ben had spotted a kebab shop with a fruit machine and no visible security, which he said would be an easy target for us. I didn't like the thought of stealing from anyone, but Ben managed to convince me that the guys running this business wouldn't care because they would be able to make a claim on their insurance for anything that we took. It wasn't like robbing someone's house, he said. I allowed myself to be talked into it, convincing myself that I wasn't actually taking anyone's personal possessions. All through my childhood Mum had taught my brothers and me that if you wanted anything in life you should just take it. She had even had us robbing from the local church collection box at one stage, until the vicar caught us and she acted as if she was shocked and mortified by our actions. So although I did have a conscience squeaking away in the back of my head, I took no notice of it, telling myself this was just the way things were, that everyone was the same and that if I didn't join in I was being stupid. I was also still feeling angry with the world for everything that had been done to me in my childhood and I was looking for a way to let the rage out, to take a bit of revenge. It was a confusing mixture of feelings, which left me vulnerable to Ben and his manipulating ways.

The kebab shop was deserted and locked up like everything else. It wasn't hard to kick out the bottom panel of the back door and then we were inside. Ben and Jock seemed to know exactly what they were doing as they broke into the fruit machine with a steel bar and scooped out handfuls of jangling coins. I had never seen so much money in one place. We filled our pockets until they were bulging, and then Ben told me to hold out the hem of my tracksuit top to make a cradle, so that he could fill that too. I could hardly move for fear of dropping the coins and I wondered if there might be a silent alarm going off in a police station somewhere and the cops would be waiting for us when we came out. There wasn't much chance I could deny anything with so much of the evidence clutched to me, and I didn't think I would be speedy enough to outrun anyone unless I dropped the lot.

Coins were spilling out and rolling away as we crawled back out of the hole in the door and scurried home as quickly as we could, laughing and joking as we went. We divided the money up between us on the kitchen table and I gave my share to Lisa. I think it came to about fifty quid each. Looking back now, of course I can see that I was stealing in order to feed her drink habit, but at the time I was just a sixteen-year-old kid in love, who wanted to please the people who were taking care of him and making him feel better about himself. Despite her previous reservations, Lisa seemed impressed by what I had done for her, and her approval made me feel even better about myself.

Having been reluctant to have anything to do with the venture at first, I was now buzzing with adrenaline and bouncing around with excitement, wanting to go straight back out and repeat the experience.

'Whoa, mate,' Ben said, laughing at my youthful exuberance. 'That's enough for one night. Maybe tomorrow we'll get you doing a bit of smash and grab.'

Smash and grab? I wasn't sure what he was talking about, but it sounded both scary and exciting. One part of me was raring to go, while the voice at the back of my head was warning me that I was slipping out of my depth and about to get into serious trouble. But if I could get some more money to give to Lisa, then it was worth taking a few risks. I felt as if I had become a useful part of the squat community, as if I really belonged somewhere for the first time ever.

The next night the others taught me the rules of 'smash and grab'. The way it worked was that we would line up in front of a chosen shop with a brick each and we just kept hurling those bricks at the toughened glass until it started to crack. The moment a crack appeared we would keep battering at that weak spot. If the window didn't break within a few seconds, we would make a run for it, because the alarms would always be going by then and we knew we only had a couple of minutes before the police arrived. In most cases the windows would go quickly and we would be in, grabbing what we wanted from the displays and shelves, cramming it into empty bags that we had brought with us. We would be back out of the window and away again within a minute. It was amazing how much stuff you could snatch up in sixty seconds. Mostly it was jeans, jumpers and shirts that would be easy for Ben to sell in the pubs and to friends.

As long as I ignored the little voice telling me I was stealing, the smash-and-grab raids were a real buzz and for a while we went out filling our bags virtually every night. There was one poor retailer in particular whom we used to hit over and over again. Every time they mended their window we would be back there a week or two later and the manager would have to be called back out again in the middle of the night to deal with the alarm and make the shop secure again until morning. We used to walk past later sometimes and see him slaving away, and I still feel guilty about that poor guy to this day.

At the time it never seemed as if we were attacking anyone personally because those empty, night-time shopping precincts appeared inhuman, just part of a cold, empty, hostile landscape. Having got a taste for the excitement, and often becoming bored sitting around in the house when the others were all too drunk or high to make any sense, I started to go out with Jake pretty much every night, as we used to do when we were in London. Although I didn't trust him, he was still quite good company. Everything we brought back from those raids would be passed on to Ben or Jock to get rid of and they would give us whatever money they thought we should have a few days later. Once they realized we were willing to do all the hard work for them, the two of them got lazier and lazier.

'You two go out,' they'd say. 'You're the pros.'

Stupidly, I felt quite proud to think they were willing to give me so much responsibility. The other boys did one or two house burglaries in the area as well and asked me to go with them, but I never did.

'What if they've got kids?' Lisa asked them when they first suggested it, and I could immediately imagine that these houses might have children living in them. I could picture exactly how they would feel when they came downstairs in the morning and discovered someone had broken into their homes while they were sleeping and had messed up their things. Even with the upbringing I'd had, I could see that that would be a wrong thing to do. What happened if one of the kids came down while we were still in the house? How traumatic would that be for them? I wanted to restrict my criminal activities to the anonymous, empty shopping streets of the town centre.

Chapter Thirteen

My Baby

Three months after I arrived at the squat, on 2 August 1989, Lisa broke the news to me that she thought she was pregnant.

'How do you know?' I asked, too shocked to even be able to take the news in properly.

'Because I'm getting fat,' she said, pinching her stomach to show me.

She said it totally casually, as if it was no big deal, but the news hit me like a sledgehammer. I had absolutely not seen it coming. How was it possible that I was going to be a dad? I was still only sixteen years old. Surely that sort of thing only happened to grown men? I knew virtually nothing about the facts of life. Maybe, I reasoned, she was just putting on a bit of weight because of all the drinking she did. We had never even discussed contraception, because I was so naïve I just assumed that girls took care of those sorts of things. She had never suggested we should use a condom or anything, so I had presumed she was on the pill or whatever it was girls did. It was easy to get condoms if you wanted – the authorities were always handing them out to people like us for free.

Working out the dates, because she said she thought she was about three months gone (although I had no idea how she knew that), it seemed that it had happened almost as soon as we got together. For a fleeting second I even wondered if I could be sure that it was my kid, but that was not a thought I would ever have dared to voice out loud and I dismissed it as ridiculous almost as soon as I thought it. I trusted Lisa completely. I knew she was always honest with me, and everyone else had always told me that she never slept with anyone in the house till I turned up.

The funny thing was she actually seemed pleased about the prospect of being a mother, which struck me as a bit odd. Did she really think either of us was ready to take on the responsibility of a baby? We couldn't even support or look after ourselves properly.

Once I had accepted that it was true and that I really was going to be a father, we worked out that the baby was due to arrive in the last week of January, and it soon became obvious that this was for real. Lisa started doing things like putting my hand on her stomach so that I could feel the baby kicking, just as millions of other proud young mums must have done before. She had me talking to it and singing to it – the whole bit. But actually I didn't mind, because it brought the two of us even closer together and I was beginning to warm to the idea of having a kid of my own. Maybe it would be a son and I would be able to be as close to him as Dad had been with me. I pictured how I would take him everywhere with me, just as Dad took me, and how I would make sure he always knew I loved him more than anything, just as Dad had always let me know.

Lisa continued happily drinking and smoking, which began to worry me, because I could imagine all that vodka and smoke going straight into the baby. I didn't know anything about human biology at all, but I couldn't believe it was a good idea to live as she did with a kid inside her. She was quite good-natured when I gave her lectures about it and she seemed to appreciate that I was only trying to be a good father and a good partner to her, and that I loved her completely; but it didn't make her change her ways. I would do anything she asked of me and in return she did promise to try to cut down on the drink and cigarettes, but I guess she was pretty badly addicted and would never have been able to just give up completely.

Although I didn't care where I was or what the living conditions were like as long as I was with Lisa, I could see that the squat wasn't the best place for anyone to bring up a baby and I began to worry about where we should go. Constantly fortified with vodka, Lisa would dismiss all my worries whenever I voiced them, assuring me something would turn up. The volunteers at the outreach centre were unhappy that she wasn't getting any neonatal care at all. They started sending a midwife round to see us, as Lisa steadfastly refused to go to them.

As she got bigger and nearer her due date, she started to talk about us leaving the area and getting away from the others to start a new life together as a little family.

'Where do you want to go then?' I asked. 'Do you want to go back to where you were brought up?'

'I don't ever want to go back there,' she said vehemently, 'because of my father. You know how I feel about him.'

I could understand that perfectly, since there was no way I would ever have wanted to go anywhere near any of my family ever again.

'So what are we going to do?' I asked.

'What if we went somewhere completely different?' she said, her eyes looking unfocused and far away. 'Like abroad?'

'I ain't even got a passport,' I pointed out. 'I don't know anything about any other country or any other languages. Do you?'

'What about Cornwall then?'

That didn't seem such a mad idea. Although I had no idea where it was, I'd heard a lot of homeless people talking about Cornwall and saying what a nice place it was.

'We could go to Penzance,' she said. 'Everyone goes there and apparently there is lots of support for homeless people.'

When we mentioned this idea to the volunteers at the outreach centre they were surprisingly positive. Maybe they thought we stood a better chance of getting our lives together if we moved away from the squat with all its bad influences. Maybe they thought there was still a chance of saving us from ourselves and from the influence of people like Ben, Jock and Jake. There was one woman volunteer who kept telling me that I shouldn't be in the squat at all.

'You're not like the others,' she would say. 'You shouldn't be homeless. You could do something with your life, Joe. It's not too late. It's never too late.'

Although I didn't really understand what she meant, because I had nowhere else to go, her words stayed in my head and made me feel better about myself; they gave me a slither of hope that one day I would actually be able to make something of my life and that I wouldn't end up living like the old tramps and alcoholics whom I ran into at the centre and whose company Jock seemed to enjoy so much. I don't know if that woman ever realized how deeply her kind words affected me, because I doubt if I showed any real response at the time. She even offered to take me in herself if I wanted, but I couldn't even think of being without Lisa and the lady wasn't willing to take her in too. Even though to me Lisa was my soulmate, maybe that woman thought she was as much of a bad influence on me as Jock, Ben and Jake.

Lisa and I enjoyed a nice Christmas in the house as a couple, even though she was getting really big and uncomfortable by then. As the due date came closer, I was increasingly excited at the thought of becoming a dad and inside my head it already felt as if there were three of us in our little family. Lisa had made Ben and Jock share a bit more of the money they were making from the things we stole for them, and despite our drink habits we had managed to save about £200 between us, which we had secreted under a loose floorboard beneath our mattress. We planned to leave for Penzance just before the baby arrived, so that the three of us could start our new life together in Cornwall.

Early one morning, a few days before we planned to leave, Lisa woke me up.

'I've got terrible pains, Joe,' she said and I could see that she was serious. Her face was a horrible pale colour and she looked drawn and frightened. 'I can't feel the baby moving.'

'Maybe it's asleep,' I said hopefully. 'They don't kick all the time, do they?'

'It doesn't feel right, Joe.' There was an edge of hysteria in her voice, which was unlike her.

'We'll go to the outreach centre,' I said. 'They'll know what to do.'

'I don't think I can move. I'm in fucking agony. I think I might need to call an ambulance.'

I knew that the others were really nervous about having anyone official coming to the squat, not wanting to draw the authorities' attention to the fact that we were there or the fact that there was stolen property all over the place waiting to be sold. Once they were in through the door, we reasoned, they would probably be able to find a way to get us out. I understood that the squat was too good a set-up for too many people for us to endanger it.

'We'll have to get outside the house before we call,' I said, and she nodded grimly. If anyone knew the score it was Lisa.

The moment I pulled back the sleeping bag to help her out we both saw the blood. It was everywhere.

'What have you done to yourself?' I shouted, panicking. Not understanding what was happening, I was frightened that I was about to lose her and the baby. 'Have you cut yourself?'

'No, I haven't.' She looked deathly pale and shocked. 'It's coming from inside me.'

I held her up and helped her to pull on some warm clothes, but the blood just kept on flowing, soaking into everything as she gripped her stomach, snapping and snarling at me as the pains dug in. She was used to being the one who made the decisions and she didn't like me telling her what to do. I didn't take it personally; I could see this was serious and I just had to keep going in order to get help. The squat was only two streets away from the outreach centre, but it felt like a hundred miles as I tried to coax her to take one more step at a time. One minute she was crying out from the pain, the next she was shouting abuse at me as I encouraged her to keep going. Her trousers were soaked with blood.

Passers-by kept asking if she was all right, but I couldn't cope with any interference. I had to concentrate on her and the baby, and I just told everyone to fuck off and leave us alone. I couldn't think what else to do and it seemed to me as if they were all trying to interfere and slow us down; I was afraid that I was in danger of losing Lisa and my baby, and in my panic these people seemed to be making the situation worse. I didn't trust any of them. I didn't know if this was what was meant to happen during a birth or if it was all going terribly wrong. I just wanted to find some familiar faces to help us. I wanted someone I trusted to tell me what I should do next, to stop Lisa's pain and bring my child safely into the world.

After what seemed like an age we reached the door of the centre. The moment the workers saw us they dialled for an ambulance and tried to calm both of us down while we waited for it for arrive. Lisa was wide eyed with fear and panting from the pain, while I was just shouting and cursing at everyone, unable to understand why everything seemed to be taking so long.

When the ambulance got there, they lifted Lisa in on her own and wouldn't let me follow. I didn't know what they were doing to her as I paced around outside, but eventually they managed to calm her screams and one of the paramedics stuck her head out the back.

'So,' she said, looking at me, 'who are you?'

'I'm her partner.'

'Right. Get in.'

I scrambled in and sat down beside Lisa, who was lying stretched out on a bed. The ambulance started to move and I felt better knowing we were on our way to the hospital. They must have done something for her pain because she was quieter and not writhing around any more. The sirens were clearing the traffic to get us there quickly. We were no longer on our own; the grown-ups had come to our rescue. It felt as if we were quite important because our baby was being born and the whole world was having to get out of our way. From being a nightmare a few minutes before it now started to feel like an adventure. I wasn't even seventeen yet and I was racing around town in an ambulance, about to become a proud father.

'It's going to be all right, lovey,' the paramedic who was sitting with us told me.

I nodded, but I couldn't understand why she needed to say that. We were just having a baby, weren't we? It was the most natural thing in the world, wasn't it? She must have been able to see that I had no real grasp of what was going on. She probably had me down as being a bit simple.

They drove us straight to the maternity section and the staff were at the doors, waiting to rush Lisa straight in. I was impressed by the way it was all working. Did all babies get this VIP treatment, I wondered? A nurse gently but firmly stopped me from following the trolley and I was ushered into a little waiting room, where a few other expectant or new fathers were sitting around, looking either proud or anxious. I felt much better now, though I was still nervous about how the birth was progressing and about the pain that I guessed Lisa was going through, wanting to be with her but assuming that this was the way things were done. I was just like these other young dads-to-be, I told myself as I settled down to wait as patiently as possible for news.

I listened to the other fathers coming and going and talking about their babies and I became more and more excited about the idea of holding my own child in my arms in a few hours' time, imagining how I was going to bond with it in the coming years. I was determined to be as good a father as my dad had been to me. My child was going to be someone I could love and who would love me, and I would be able to bring him or her up properly, not as I had been brought up after Dad was taken away from me. It might have had a bit of a bad start in life but I was going to do everything in my power to give my baby a good life from now on.

'Mr Peters?' A young doctor had come into the room and was looking for me.

'Yes?' I sprang eagerly to my feet.

'Can we have a word? Would you come into the office?'

Deep inside I felt a stirring of disquiet. The tone of the doctor's voice wasn't what I would expect from someone about to break the news that I was a proud father. I could see that the expressions on the faces of the other members of staff were all wrong, but I clung on to my dream as I followed him into the office, as if trying to will him into giving me good news. He shut the door behind me.

'I've got some bad news,' he said. 'You need to sit down.'

'Just tell me. Where's Lisa? I want to see Lisa.'

'All in good time, Joe. Please sit down.'

'Just fucking tell me!' I shouted, all my dreams draining away to be replaced by a terrible feeling of dread.

'Your baby has died.'

'How can it have died?' I didn't get it. 'Is it out?'

'No, I'm afraid it isn't out. We presume that the cord has got wrapped round its neck and strangled it.'

Nothing he was saying made any sense to me. What cord was he talking about? How could a baby be strangled before it had even taken its first breath? Why was it still inside her? I didn't get it. I just wanted to see Lisa.

I wanted to understand what was happening. I wanted to comfort her, to make things right, to show the doctor that he had got it all wrong.

He must have realized that I had no idea what he was talking about and he tried to explain what had happened, but I still couldn't bring myself to believe him. It wasn't possible that my baby was dead before I had even met it. Eventually he gave up trying to make me understand and agreed to take me through to see Lisa. I followed him in a daze, unable to take in anything that was going on around me.

When I got to her bedside I could see Lisa had been crying. There was still blood everywhere, but the doctors had gone, leaving a midwife holding her hand, trying to calm her. I just wanted to cuddle her and comfort her, but as soon as I bent over her, awkward and unsure what she would want from me, she punched me away.

'Just get out!' she screamed.

'Why are you being like that?' I couldn't understand it. Why didn't she want me to comfort her?

'Just get out. Get him out.'

The midwife gently led me away from the bed. I was even more confused now. I didn't understand anything that was happening. It was as if the whole world had gone mad around me. She led me to a little room on my own and sat me down.

'Stay here for a moment,' she said, 'while we try to calm Lisa down.'

'I don't want to stay here. I want to know what's going on. She's still got the baby in her. So it can't be dead. What's going on?'

All the fear and distrust that had lived inside me through my childhood rose to the surface. It felt as if everyone was lying to me and trying to get rid of me, and I didn't know what to do about it. A few minutes later a lady counsellor came in to talk to me. I think the doctor must have warned her that I was a bit backward for my age because she started to explain everything to me in very simple terms, as if she was talking to a child rather than a man. She explained that my baby was in Heaven, but that didn't seem right because I knew it was still in Lisa's womb. I concentrated as hard as I could on her words and as I began to understand what had happened my anger turned into an unbearable sadness and the tears began to flow. It dawned on me that I had lost my baby and I now understood that Lisa was still going to have to go through the process of giving birth. I kept asking to go and see her, but they told me she didn't want anything to do with me at the moment. They tried to explain how she was feeling and that those feelings would pass eventually.

It seemed to me that yet again God had decided to take something precious away from me. Just as He had taken away my father and then my childhood, now He had taken my baby and it felt as if I was losing Lisa as well. Why did I keep having to be punished? What had I done to make Him so angry with me?

The counsellor had been talking to Lisa as well and told me she had explained to her that I was grieving too. Eventually Lisa said she was willing to see me and for a short time she seemed to soften her attitude towards me. Maybe they had given her some medication to calm her down. I felt better when I was with her, telling myself that whatever happened, at least we still had each other.

Late that night they induced the birth and Lisa agreed to let me be in the delivery room with her so that I could go through the birth process too. The counsellor said that would be important for me. The pain of the contractions must have been terrible and all I could do was hold Lisa's hand and try to think of something to say that might bring her some comfort. As the pain built up, she flew into a rage and screamed at me to get out of the room, saying it was all my fault, grabbing my hair as I leant forward and biting me. The counsellor was there too, trying to reason with her and put my point of view, saying that we needed to be together for the birth of our child, but I was beginning to think that maybe Lisa was right: maybe it was all my fault.

Eventually the staff decided she was becoming too distressed and I had to leave the delivery room. It was past ten o'clock by then and dark outside the windows of the almost silent hospital. I slumped down in the waiting room, exhausted by the stress of the day and the hopelessness of everything. All the will to fight had drained out of me. About an hour later the doctor came back in to find me.

'You've had a baby boy,' he said.

'Can I see him, and Lisa?' I asked quietly.

'Lisa is being sedated,' he explained. 'She was in a bit of a state. Can you wait a little while for us to clean the baby up before you see him?'

He went out again and I paced up and down the room, waiting to be told when I could go through, crying. Part of me was desperate to see him while another part was frightened of how painful it was going to be. I still wondered if perhaps they had made a mistake and I would be holding him and he would suddenly cry and take a breath and be alive.

The counsellor eventually took me to a room with a cot standing in the corner. I stood in the middle of the room, frozen, staring at my feet, too scared to look over. The counsellor picked him up and brought him to me. I wasn't sure that I wanted to hold him, or whether I would be able to cope with the emotions that would unleash.

'Sit down, Joe,' she said, nodding towards the chair, placing him in my arms wrapped in a yellow blanket. Taking a deep breath, I lifted the corner of the blanket. They had dressed him for me and he looked beautiful, so perfect and tiny. It didn't seem possible that he wasn't alive. I stared at his little fingers, unable to believe that this was my son and he had gone from me already.

Chapter Fourteen

The Aftermath

An explosion of noise interrupted my thoughts, making me jump. Alarms were going off all over the hospital and a midwife came bustling in.

'We have to put Baby back now,' she commanded, 'and I have to ask you to go back to the waiting room, Mr Peters.'

'I think Mr Peters needs to hold his baby for a little longer,' the counsellor told her, but the midwife wasn't having it.

'No,' she said firmly. 'We need to put him back and take Mr Peters to the other room.'

I didn't know what the alarm was all about, but everyone seemed to be rushing around in a panic and I didn't know what to say. The counsellor seemed to realize she had been overruled and gently took the tiny bundle from me, wrapped him back up in his blanket and placed him in the cot. The midwife was so fierce and bossy that she reignited all the anger that always lurked beneath the surface inside me, reminding me how much I hated having my life dictated to me by other people, especially women who reminded me of my mother.

'You fucking bitch!' I shouted at her as the counsellor led me out. 'You can't stop me from holding my baby!'

But she could and she did, leaving me feeling impotent and vulnerable. Back in the waiting room on my own I had no idea what was happening or what I should do next. Should I go and look for Lisa? Should I have insisted on holding my baby for longer or should I just walk away from the whole thing and come back again tomorrow? Only later did I discover that the alarms had gone off because Lisa had woken from her sedated state feeling so miserable that she had smashed a glass and slashed her own throat with the jagged edge. The staff were having to put all their efforts into restraining her, which was why they needed to ensure I was nowhere near by to cause any more trouble. I knew none of this. All I knew was I had only been given a couple of minutes with my dead baby and now I was being ordered around by people I didn't know and who didn't seem to like me.

Once they had got control of Lisa, the medical staff's next objective must have been to get me out of the hospital quickly in case I somehow upset her again. They came to the waiting room to tell me I had to go but they wouldn't tell me why. I suppose they thought that if I knew what Lisa had done I would start trying to rush into her room. I pleaded with them to tell me what was going on. I begged them to let me see Lisa, but all they would say was she had hurt herself and that she needed to talk to a psychiatrist before I could see her again.

'Go home now and get some sleep,' a nurse told me, 'and come back again tomorrow. We'll be able to tell you more then.'

I didn't want to leave the hospital as long as Lisa and the baby were still in there. I wanted to be with them. I wanted to hold my baby again. The counsellor seemed to be the only one on my side but she didn't seem to be able to get through to anyone any more than I could. Once I was outside in the dark I felt completely alone and lost in the world. There was nowhere for me to go but back to the squat.

By the time I got there it was about one o'clock in the morning. Everyone else in the house was awake and seemed to know more about what had happened to us than I did. I guess the people at the outreach centre had been phoning the hospital or something. They were all trying to comfort and cuddle me, but I didn't want to be touched. I needed to be comforted but I didn't know how to accept sympathy, having experienced so little of it through my life. I felt angry and suspicious and worried and frightened and lonely and desperate. The whole world seemed such a hostile, cruel place. I couldn't understand why even Lisa had turned against me after

131

all we had been through together in the previous nine months. I had thought she was my soulmate and that we were going to start a family and spend the rest of our lives together, and now she had pushed me away and I was on my own again. I couldn't sort it out in my head; I couldn't work out how I was going to cope with the pain I was feeling at finding myself rejected yet again.

'Leave him alone,' Jake told the others as they fussed around me. 'Let him mellow out.'

Grateful to him for understanding what I needed, I went into our bedroom to have a few moments alone. Lisa's blood was still on the sleeping bag, which lay in the same place we had dropped it when we had rushed from the house that morning. I sank down on to the mattress and cried and cried, thumping the walls with my fists, kicking out at everything that was in my way like a small child in the grip of a tantrum. There was a bottle of vodka tucked down beside the mattress and I drank deeply, trying in vain to numb the pain. The walls seemed to be closing in on me and I didn't want to talk to any of the others. Everything about the house reminded me of Lisa and of how happy she had made me feel over the previous nine months. Unable to stand it for another moment and knowing that I wouldn't be able to sleep even if I tried, I stormed back out into the night.

Jake saw me going and came running after me.

'Fuck off and leave me alone,' I shouted as I ran down the street.

'I'm not letting you go off on your own,' he said firmly. 'I won't bother you.'

Although I didn't want to have him around me, I couldn't help but be touched that he was concerned about me. He might have been a treacherous little bastard in the past, but he was at least trying to act like a friend now. Without saying anything else I ran off and he followed a few paces behind, giving me space but keeping an eye on me. My anger was completely out of control and when I reached the town centre I ran from one shop window to the next, hurling bricks and flower-pots, smashing everything I could lay my hands on. I didn't steal anything; I just wanted to take it out on the world. I didn't care what happened to me at that moment.

My rage was beginning to abate as I heard the distant sound of sirens. They were growing louder, coming closer.

'Run,' Jake shouted, and I noticed he was carrying his bag with him. Maybe he had been planning to pick up a few things, but it looked empty as he sprinted away down the streets, so he must have thought better of it. I ran after him, not wanting to get arrested that night on top of everything else.

Once we were a few streets away from the scene of devastation that I had caused, we slowed down to a walk. The sudden burst of exercise had left me panting and feeling slightly calmer.

'Do you want to go back to the squat now then?' Jake asked.

'No,' I shook my head. 'I don't want to go back yet.'

I felt I needed the quiet and the fresh air. I wasn't ready to bury myself back behind the boarded-up windows yet. I wanted to try to straighten my thoughts out and work out what was going on inside my head. We walked on for a while, talking a bit now and then. Then Jake noticed that the lace had come undone on one of his trainers and was trailing in the dirt.

'Hold this a second,' he said, passing me his empty bag before crouching down to retie it.

I waited for him, looking around, and that was the moment that I saw the police car creeping round the corner and drawing up at the kerb. Two cops got out of the car and came over to us. I'd been stopped and searched before when I'd been out and about late at night. Luckily they had never come across me when I was carrying anything. I knew I was clean that night and I couldn't see how they could pin the broken windows on me, since we were a good few streets away by then. I took a deep breath and prepared myself for the usual pantomime.

'Fuck off, copper!' I growled as one of them came over, the other one standing a little way back, watching and waiting to see what would happen and whether he would need to intervene. 'I ain't done nothing.'

'You won't mind it I stop and search you then,' he said.

'What for?'

'There's been some incidents in the town and we just need to check you out. We can take you into the station if you prefer or we can do it the easy way and I can search you now.'

I shrugged. I didn't care much either way any more. I dropped Jake's bag on the floor and lifted my arms up to let him pat me down. Once he'd done that he picked up the bag.

'Mind if I look in here?' he asked.

'It's not my bag,' I said.

'You were holding it.'

'I was just holding it for him.' I nodded towards Jake, who was staying strangely quiet.

'It's not my bag,' Jake said.

'What are you on about?' I asked, still not really taking in what was happening.

'It's not my bag,' he insisted.

'Oh, just search it,' I said, tired of the whole business. 'There's nothing in there anyway. It's empty.'

It might have felt empty, but in fact there was a single pair of jeans neatly folded inside the bag, left over from a burglary Jake had done a few nights before. They still had their security tag on. Jake had stitched me up yet again. He had been pretending to care about me and be my friend and the moment the chips were down he was framing me to save his own skin. I couldn't believe it. I called him every name under the sun, ranting and screaming at him.

'How can you do this?' I wanted to know. 'You know what I've been through tonight already.'

But he kept the innocent act up without a blink of conscience. The second copper must have been able to see that I was in a dangerous mood and stepped forward to provide back-up as his mate went to handcuff us. Jake put his hands out, good as gold, but I wasn't ready to give up that easily and wriggled free. I tried to make a run for it, but they were too fast for me and one of them caught me halfway up the road while his colleague put Jake into the car. Once he had a grip of me he didn't take any chances, throwing me on to the ground on my face and cuffing my hands behind my back.

'Just fucking calm down,' he said, his fingers round my throat as he dragged me back to the car and pushed me in next to Jake. It seemed a bit excessive to me, but I guess I seemed like trouble and he didn't know what I had been through that day. I suppose it looked to him as if I was the one trying to blame my mate for my crimes rather than the other way round. It was all so unfair that I just wanted to scream. Being locked in the back of a car yet again made me panic all the more. What were they going to do to me once they got me to the station? How was I going to be able to get back to the hospital in the morning to see the baby before they took him away if they were going to lock me up? I was becoming more and more desperate as the coppers got into the front seats and started to drive. I was kicking at Jake and at the door, lashing out without any idea of what I hoped to achieve. I was completely out of control and the driver stamped on the brake, while his mate came round to the back to sort me out.

The moment he opened the door and bent down to grab me I managed to kick him hard in the face, sending him sprawling backwards. Recovering himself, he lunged back, grabbed me and pulled me out of the car, throwing me back down on the ground while his mate radioed for back-up and for a van to take me in to the station.

By the time a couple more police cars turned up, and then a van, the policeman I'd kicked was coming up with a nasty black eye and the others taped my ankles together so that I couldn't kick out again and damage anyone else. They were obviously pissed off with me, giving me the odd punch and kick as I wriggled and struggled and made their lives as difficult as I could.

'Little bastard,' the first kept saying, dabbing gingerly at his eye.

Once they had me safely trussed up, they lifted me bodily and swung me into the back of the van like a sack of potatoes.

When we got to the station, they carried me out and into the custody suite, straight past the sergeant and into a cell. I suppose they could tell I was not in a mood to give anyone my name and details, so they didn't bother to waste their time even asking. Once I was in the cell, they finally undid my wrists and ankles and left me to cool down, slamming the door behind them as I screamed and yelled abuse at them like some mad caged animal, locked in a cell yet again with all the hideous memories that brought back. I was head-butting the door and going mad, shouting at Jake in the next cell, telling him I was going to kill him when I got my hands on him. I must have sounded like a right nutter.

The police later told their boss they came into the cell because they were worried I was going to injure myself, but in reality I suspect they had just had enough and wanted to shut me up and teach me a lesson. I lost count of how many of them came bursting in through the door to give me a punching and a kicking, led by the man I had given the black eye to. I fought back like a wild thing, not caring any more about the conse-quences, but I didn't stand a chance against so many grown men. It was all a blur of pain and blows, but through it all I saw an older man come in behind the others.

'All right,' he said loudly, 'that's enough. Out!'

By the time they had all left the cell I was lying in a heap with a good few of my teeth missing. But I was still shouting abuse at them, and looking back now I have to confess I probably deserved that hiding. I was being a right pain, even though I couldn't see it at the time. I had pushed my luck too far. I had also made things a hundred times worse for myself. I was desperate to get back to Lisa and to hold my baby boy again to say good-bye, and if I had just cooperated with the police a bit that night maybe things would have gone better the follow-ing day.

Chapter Fifteen

Nowhere to Go

I didn't sleep much that night. I just stared around the cell, lost in my own thoughts, trying to work out what I should do. There was graffiti scratched into the paintwork of the door, and glass bricks had been set high up in the wall to allow at least a little light to infiltrate from outside. At six o'clock the cell door opened again and an inspector came in. I recognized him as the man who had called the others off me a few hours before. He was older than the men who had beaten me up, as well as more senior.

'Right, Mr Peters,' he said. 'Have you calmed down now?'

'Yeah,' I said, and then I spat a mixture of phlegm and blood in his face. 'Now I'm calm, you bastard.'

'There was no need for that,' he said, wiping his eye.

'Fuck off, pig!'

He nodded his understanding of the situation and walked calmly out, closing the door firmly but softly behind him. I thought he had gone to send the others back in to give me another going over, but nothing happened. About an hour later he tried again, talking through the hatch.

'If I come in,' he said, 'are you just going to spit at me or can we talk sensibly?'

I appreciated the fact that he hadn't sent his officers back in. 'Whatever,' I said. 'Do what you like. I just want to get out of here.'

'OK. Sit back down on the bench then.'

Once I was safely sat down he opened the door and came in, obviously wary in case I went off on one again.

'I've got something for you to eat and drink.' He put a cup and plate down. 'I'm just putting it down there. OK?'

'Whatever.'

He stood back and looked at me. 'Do you want to see a doctor?'

'No.'

'OK. I'll be back in a minute. If you want anything else, just press the buzzer.'

I couldn't understand why he was being so nice to me when a few hours before they had been beating me up. I didn't trust any of them. I looked down at the plate. There was a piece of bread and some scrambled egg. I was hungry, so I took a mouthful, spitting it back out again immediately. It was the most disgusting thing I had ever tasted, even worse than the stuff Mum and my brothers used to make me lick up off the floor. The inspector came back half an hour later.

'Weren't you hungry?' he asked, glancing at the abandoned food.

'It was the most disgusting shit I've ever tasted.'

'Ah,' he smiled. 'Our chef isn't in yet, I'm afraid. One of the officers made it.'

I felt pretty sure that if that was the case there would have been more ingredients than eggs in the mix. No wonder it had tasted so foul. Now that he could see I had calmed down, he told me to follow him and we went through to the custody sergeant to get my details taken down. The sergeant was one of the men who had beaten me up in the early hours.

'I want to complain about him,' I said as soon as I saw him. 'He was one of the ones who gave me a hiding.'

'We'll worry about that later, shall we?' the inspector said. 'Let's just get this sorted. If you prefer, I'll process you myself.'

He went round the desk and the sergeant stepped back.

'What's your address?'

'I live in a squat,' I told him, giving the address.

'You can't put that,' he said. 'We have to say "no fixed abode".'

'What's an *abode*?' I asked, exaggerating the word but genuinely curious.

'The place you live,' he said patiently.

'But I have got a "fixed abode". I've lived there nearly a year.'

'No, you are there illegally. You don't pay any rent or anything.'

'Whatever.'

He had to take my picture as well and I kept messing about, pulling faces and flicking a finger at the camera. He was amazingly patient considering how cheeky I was being and how I was wasting his time.

'Come on,' he said wearily. 'Do this properly, lad. This is going on the record and you don't want to look like an idiot, do you?'

'Who's going to see it?'

'The courts maybe, and police intelligence.'

He was so reasonable, as if he was actually trying to help me, that I started doing what he said.

'We're charging you with criminal damage and four thefts,' he said.

I didn't know why he had decided on the figure of four, but I couldn't be bothered to argue.

'I suppose you're going to charge me with hitting the coppers as well,' I sneered.

'No,' he said.

That shut me up. I realized that he was offering me a deal. If I didn't complain about the coppers, they wouldn't charge me with assault. Thankfully, I was calm enough by then to realize that it was a good deal for me, so I kept quiet. If they were just going to charge me with the thefts, maybe I would be able to get out quicker than I had feared and get to the hospital in time to see my baby again. Once I was logged in, they got me a duty solicitor and interviewed me. They told me that I could have a copy of the recording as well if I wanted.

'Yeah,' I said, wanting to put them to as much trouble as possible. 'I'll have one of them.'

The solicitor read the papers once they were prepared.

'They are charging you with "crimes to be taken into consideration",' he said.

'What are you on about?'

'Let's not worry about that at the moment. I suggest you cooperate with the police.'

All the way through the interview I answered almost every question 'no comment', which was what Ben and Jock had always said we should do if we were ever caught for anything. That way the police couldn't bend our words and use them against us in court or against one another at a later date. The policemen doing the interview told me they had interviewed Jake and that he had told them all the robberies were down to me. I was pretty sure that they were trying to catch me out, although I wouldn't have put anything past Jake on his past performance.

'He's a fucking liar,' was all I said, before going back to 'no comment'.

I guess Jake must have given the impression that he was cooperating with them while I was being a complete pain in the arse. They needed to find a ringleader, someone to blame, and it must have seemed obvious to them that I was the best candidate for the job. I kept telling them that the bag with the jeans in wasn't mine, but they obviously didn't believe me and I suppose as far as they were concerned I was as likely to be lying as Jake. They decided to raid the squat to see what else they could find. They thought about taking me with them when they went, but decided against it because of the way I had behaved in the cell and during my arrest the previous day. I guess they thought they would have to spend all their time restraining me instead of searching and dealing with anyone else they came across. Apparently there was no legal requirement for me to be there, since I didn't legally live there.

So I had to wait in the cell, not knowing what was going on, fretting all the time about the hours that were ticking away, during which I was still not able to see Lisa or the baby. Every time I got to see the inspector I was begging him to let me go to the hospital. I knew it was no use asking any of the others for any mercy.

'We can't do that yet, son,' he kept saying. 'I'm sorry.'

He did, however, agree to make a call to the hospital on my behalf to find out what was going on.

'They've had to section your girlfriend,' he told me, 'under the Mental Health Act because she is a danger to herself, so she won't be coming out any time soon.'

He went on to tell me the details about her trying to cut her own throat with the broken glass, which explained why the alarms had gone off while I was there and why everyone was running around. The things he told me just made me want to be with Lisa all the more, to help her and comfort her and reassure her that I would always be there for her. I could imagine how terrible she was feeling at being left on her own, because that was exactly how I was feeling, locked in my cell while the police and the hospital staff and everyone else went about their business and decided on my fate.

'We'll get you into court first thing Monday morning,' the inspector said (it was then Friday), 'or at least the day after. We'll ask for bail, but we'll have to fix you up with a bail hostel before there's any chance they will grant that.'

There was no option for me other than to be patient and endure the agonizing wait to see what happened next. Later I discovered that on the raid the police arrested every single one of my housemates. They took out countless sacks of stolen goods and everyone told them that it was all down to me. The police now seemed to be forming the opinion that I was responsible for virtually every smash and grab that had happened in the area over the previous six months.

'We hardly had any of these crimes in this area till you turned up,' the inspector told me. 'Once you showed the way other people started jumping on the band-wagon. You started your own little crime wave.'

'Really?' This didn't sound too good.

'We reckon,' he went on, 'that you and your mates are responsible for about seventy per cent of the crimes against "non-dwelling" properties in the city over the last half year.'

I was amazed. I had never thought of it in those terms at all. I thought it was just a few pairs of jeans and a few shirts. I didn't see myself as a serious career criminal.

When I finally got into court on the Monday, the Crown Prosecution Service asked to have me remanded in custody because of the number of crimes I had been accused of. Apparently no one had been able to find a bail hostel that was willing or able to take me, so there was no chance of any bail and I was taken down to the police cells beneath the courts and left there. I was still only sixteen and I really didn't have much idea of what was going on around me as everyone tried to find some-where for me to be taken to.

Chapter Sixteen

Prison

After hours of waiting, my lawyer told me that I was going to be taken to Lewes prison, a Category A establishment for hardened criminals, despite the fact that I was only sixteen. Everyone who heard that that was where I was going looked surprised and double-checked that a mistake hadn't been made. There hadn't, and the more shock I saw on people's faces the more terrified I became.

All I knew about this place was what I heard other people saying and I didn't like the sound of it at all. It triggered all my worst fears. Once again I was going to have my freedom taken away. I was going to be locked in a cell, just as I had been for so much of my childhood, and I was going to be surrounded by hard, violent adult men. I assumed many of them would be murderers and rapists and child abusers – exactly the sort of men who had attacked and tortured me in the past. It was as if I was about to be transported back to my own private hell, and this time my imprisonment was going to be officially sanctioned by the legal establishment. There was no one else I could turn to and beg for help, no one I could believe might come galloping to my assistance.

Once they had decided where they were going to dump me, I was handcuffed and led out to a waiting prison van. The back doors were swung open and I was escorted in and guided into one of the tiny, confined cubicles that kept each prisoner separate. The door of the cubicle was slammed shut and locked, and I sat listening to the swearing and shouting of the other prisoners as they were put behind the other doors, swapping news on what had happened to them in court and talking about the place we were about to be driven to. I was trembling with fear at the thought of what might lie in wait for me at the end of the journey.

In the privacy of that cubicle I started to cry like a baby, blaming myself for my own stupidity almost as much as I blamed Jake for framing me so blatantly to save his own skin. I'd been told that he had been bailed, along with all my other housemates from the squat, and the police had found somewhere for him to go. If I hadn't been so aggressive and angry and unreasonable, they would almost certainly have been able to do the same for me. It looked as though I was going to be carrying the can for the crimes of the whole house, as though I was some sort of gangster or criminal mastermind, and

I realized now that it was partly my own fault for being so uncooperative with the police. I thought of Lisa and our baby in the hospital and the longing to get to them was like a physical ache.

The first thing that happened when we were delivered to the forbidding-looking prison and unloaded from our cubicles was a strip search. Standing virtually naked and being frisked before being given the standard issue prison outfit brought back a thousand memories of being at the mercy of grown men and again I dreaded to think what lay in store for me once I was inside.

'How old are you?' one of the screws asked, looking back and forth between me and my paperwork, obviously finding it hard to believe that I was even sixteen, given my skinny frame and baby face.

'Sixteen,' I said, trying to keep the tremble of tears out of my voice and sounding more aggressive than I should in the circumstances.

'What's this little lad doing here?' the screw asked one of his colleagues, obviously not bothered by my tone. I guess they were used to dealing with tougher men than me. They'd seen it all before and must have realized that I was terrified.

Everyone was puzzled and shrugging, but they kept on processing me through the system, following the orders of the court.

'Governor wants to see you,' I was told once all the formalities were over.

I followed the screw as instructed, too frightened now to be giving anyone any of the backchat that I had been indulging in at the police station. This screw seemed quite a fair guy, a tough ex-soldier covered in tattoos. I discovered he was called Matt.

'I can't believe a kid like you is in a place like this,' he said as he marched me towards the governor's office.

There was a woman typing in an outer office, shooting curious looks across the room as I came in.

'You don't sit down unless the governor tells you,' Matt instructed as we paused, 'and don't speak unless you're spoken to.'

I nodded my understanding and he knocked on the door. A deep voice told us to enter. The governor looked me up and down and told Matt to stay in the room. I expect he had been told that I was liable to lose my temper and could be violent, although as far as I was concerned I had only ever been defending myself.

'So, Joe,' he said, thumbing through the paperwork on the desk in front of him, 'you've been making a bit of a nuisance of yourself, haven't you?'

'What do you mean?' I said, sharply.

'Did I ask you to speak?' he said sharply, looking up at me over his glasses, and I could almost hear the exasperated breath escaping from Matt's lungs. I glanced at him and he shook his head in warning.

'I'm not happy with you being sent here,' the governor went on, 'but apparently there is no space for you anywhere else and we'll have to make the best of the situation.'

He went on to tell me a bit about the prison and how I would be wise to keep my head down and not cause any trouble.

'Keep yourself to yourself,' he warned. 'Don't get involved with anyone. Prisoners have to share cells here because we're overcrowded, but if a single cell comes up I'll try to make sure you get it.'

On the outside I pretended that I didn't care about any of it, as if I was hard enough to handle whatever they threw at me, but my insides had turned to jelly when I thought about who I might have to share a cell with, imagining it might be a man like Max or Uncle Douglas or Amani.

'I know you're nervous,' he went on, obviously seeing right through my 'tough guy' act. 'I would be at your age. We'll put you on A Wing, which is where the less violent men go.'

He was thumbing through lists of prisoners to try to find me a cellmate who he thought would be suitable while I continued to try to look as if I wasn't bothered and fought to stop myself from shaking.

'Ah, we seem to be full on A Wing.' He looked momentarily perturbed. 'Well, this chap has been a pain, so we'll temporarily move him to B Wing and let you have his bunk.'

Getting someone thrown out of the non-violent wing so that I could have a bunk didn't seem like the best start possible. It seemed to me there would now be people resenting me before I even arrived.

As Matt marched me off to my designated cell, we went through what seemed like endless sets of bars and gates that he opened with his clanking set of keys, and into a recreation area where prisoners were playing snooker, smoking or watching the fuzzy picture of a little portable television. They all looked up as I came in. A female screw announced my name and gave me a piece of card which had all my details and what I was in for, and which was going to be posted outside my cell. I could see that all the prisoners were shocked by how young I looked, nudging one another and whispering.

My cellmate was lying on his bunk as I followed Matt in through the door. He looked as if he was in his early twenties. I didn't want to say anything, for fear that I might say the wrong thing and get a beating the moment Matt had left us, but the other guy was pretty friendly and chatted away, asking what I was in for.

'Who did you kill?'

'I didn't kill anyone,' I said. 'Just did a few smash and grabs.'

He seemed to lose interest and changed the subject. I was only in there a few hours before Matt came back to tell me I was moving to another cell. The governor must have decided to have a word with the hardest man on the wing, a Scotsman called Frank, and had asked him if he would keep an eye on me. Frank, who I would guess was in his forties, must have agreed and I was told to move to his cell. He was inside for killing his girlfriend and attacking some man she had been playing around with. Half the time he would admit to me that he was guilty; then he would deny it and say it was an accident and he was innocent. I soon learned that everyone in prison always claims they're innocent and I got some funny looks when I happily confessed to my misdemeanours, as if I had broken some secret prison code.

Frank gave me a wry look as I came into the cell. 'You're nothing but a wee boy, aren't you?' he said once Matt had left us. 'What's a wee boy like you doing in here?'

It was as if he was ticking me off for being a bad boy, like an indulgent old uncle. There was something about him, though, which told me not to give him back any cheek. To be honest, I pretty quickly realized how valuable it was going to be to have him by my side, since everyone obviously respected him. When we went out of the cell to socialize, he actually warned the others off touching me.

'If any of these fuckers give you any trouble,' he said, 'you tell me.'

It wasn't long before I realized just how protected I was with Frank on my side and I returned to my cocky form, giving everyone except him a lot of backchat, knowing that I was safe. Most of them could probably see that I had issues and that I shouldn't have been in a place like that and were willing to leave me alone, but I could see there were some who were itching to take me down a peg or two and if they had ever managed to get me on my own I would have been in big trouble, so I stuck close to Frank at all times, like a faithful little puppy. My antics seemed to amuse him most of the time.

'He's looking at me funny, Frank,' I would say, just to make mischief for someone I didn't like the look of. 'Give him a hiding.'

'Behave yourself,' he would chuckle whenever I started to get gobby.

I was in there for my seventeenth birthday in March and a lot of the inmates made cards for me and even sang 'Happy Birthday'. As I relaxed amongst them I gradually became less aggressive and started to respect them all. Slowly but surely I was learning the advantages of trying to get along with other people rather than always looking for trouble.

The worst thing was missing Lisa and never being allowed to see or hold the baby again. I heard there was going to be a little funeral for him and I asked Matt if I would be allowed to go on compassionate grounds. He asked for me, but the answer came back as no. It made me sad to think he had gone completely from the earth and I had only been able to spend those few short minutes with him in my arms. He had been taken away from me just as brutally as my dad had been and it seemed like one more demonstration of how unfair life could be. It didn't seem fair on him either, not to have his dad at his funeral.

Chapter Seventeen

My Kind Defender

My court hearing wasn't until the middle of April, by which time I had been in Lewes prison for two months and staring at four walls was really beginning to get to me, pressing in on my mind like a vice. To relieve the frustration and anger, I started cutting myself, just as I had seen Lisa doing back at the squat. Now I could understand exactly why she, and so many other desperate young people, wanted to harm themselves: how it relieved the tension and vented some of the anger and hatred I felt towards myself. Matt said the authorities were talking about sending me to the prison hospital, but Frank spoke up for me and talked them out of it.

'Leave him with me,' he told Matt. 'I'll keep an eye on him.'

They agreed to his suggestion, although they put me on suicide watch, which meant officers would look through the spyhole into the cell every hour to check that

157

I was OK. I got fed up with being watched and stuck a piece of toilet paper over the inside of the hole.

'You'll get into trouble for that,' Frank said, sighing, when he saw what I was doing. 'Take it down.'

'Fuck 'em,' I said. 'They're only screws.'

He just shook his head like a tolerant but despairing parent.

'You'll just get more days on the end of your sentence if you wind them up. It won't go in your favour.'

I knew he was right, but I was so bored and hyped up I was unable to control my impulses much of the time. Unable to sleep, I kept pressing the buzzer in the night and waking the screws up, just for the hell of it. It was partly boredom, partly bravado and partly because I just didn't know any better. Matt had been made my prison liaison officer and I had managed to build a relationship with him, as I had with Frank. They both gave me serious talkings to and I took in some of what they were saying. I guess they were both having to make up for more than ten years of me lacking a father figure. If my dad had still been alive I would probably never have ended up in that state because he would have steered me in the right directions. I knew that and I was grateful to both of the men for caring enough to try to show me the error of my ways, even though I didn't intend to show either of them that I was taking any notice.

Matt spent a lot of time with me, coaxing me to tell him more about my past, taking me into his office, which someone had tried to make look less threatening by putting curtains up at the window to hide the bars. To begin with I didn't want to tell him any more than he already knew. It was embarrassing to tell other men about the things that had been done to me; to admit that my own mother had hated me so much she had locked me up for years and then sold me to other men who abused me in the most horrible ways imaginable. I didn't want to remember, either, the way my brothers and my stepfather had raped and tortured me all those years, because it was humiliating and showed the world how little my own family cared for me. But Matt knew that if the courts were told a bit about my past they would be more likely to understand how I had got myself into the mess I was now in. Smashing a few shop windows and snatching a few pairs of jeans would be more understandable acts, he explained, if people realized what state of mind I was in when I did it.

I'm sure Matt had heard stories like mine before; virtually every runaway kid on the streets is escaping from his or her family and the vast majority have been abused physically, mentally and sexually. When you added on the pressure I was under with Lisa and the baby, however, he said he thought that the courts were likely to be much more understanding about the crime spree that they believed I had been on.

He made me endless cups of tea and chatted to me in such a friendly way that I eventually mellowed and began to give him a glimpse into the hell that had been my life from five onwards. I still didn't go into that much detail, but there was enough there for me to see his eyebrows going up once or twice.

'You deserve a break, Joe,' he said eventually. 'You shouldn't even be in a prison. I promise you I'm going to do all I can to get you out of here. The first thing we have to do is tell the governor a bit about what you have been telling me. That will mean I need you to give me permission to break your confidence. And we need to call the police in to investigate your abusers.'

'What the fuck are you on about?' I was horrified. The police were the last people I wanted to be involved with. They'd beaten me up and thrown me into prison. Why would I want to tell them any more about myself? I was scared of them, just as I was scared of every other authority figure. 'Why would you want to do that?'

'What you've told me is very distressing. These people need to be held accountable for what they did to you. They were meant to be looking after you. There have been offences committed here, Joe. Given everything that has happened to you, you shouldn't be in here. You should just be given a caution and let out. They're the ones who should be in prison.'

I didn't believe him and I felt a twinge of panic at the thought of Mum and Amani and the rest of them finding out I had grassed on them. Had I talked too much? Had I made a mistake in letting my guard down? Had

Matt tricked me into trusting him, only to betray me as everyone else had in the past?

'It was the pigs who put me in this place,' I shouted. 'I don't want anything to do with them. I'll deny it all. Don't even think about it.'

He took no notice of my protests and went to the governor with the whole story. The governor then called me into his office to ask me about it. But I had learned my lesson by then and I wasn't saying another word.

'There's no point us calling the police in to take his statement,' the governor said to Matt eventually, 'if he won't even speak to us.'

On the morning of the Crown Court hearing everyone at the prison was convinced they were seeing the back of me. Frank and the others were sure a judge would listen to my story and realize I was in the wrong place.

'Get your bag packed,' Matt said when he came for me. 'You won't be coming back. I'm going to see to that.'

Bubbling with excitement, I gave Frank a proper hug before leaving the cell – something I would never have been able to imagine myself doing a few months before.

'You're going to be all right,' he said, patting me on the back. 'Let's not see you back in here, lad. You're not one of us.'

Matt was determined that I should make a good impression on the judge and jury and even sorted out a shirt and jacket for me to wear, ignoring my sullen protests. Once I got there, I could see why he had thought I should dress up, since it was the full Crown Court scene, with men wearing wigs and gowns and talking in big booming voices that echoed round the panelled walls. The posh bloke from the Crown Prosecution Service read out all the charges, reciting all the dates and details. They were basically accusing me of doing every non-dwelling robbery that had occurred in the city over the previous two years, even though I hadn't been living there that long. The total came to 465 charges of criminal theft and damage. He made it sound as if I was the criminal mastermind, as if they had managed to catch the top man of some organized crime syndicate. He also mentioned that I had assaulted a police officer, although the police didn't want to press charges on that one.

My QC applied for bail.

'How old is your client?' the judge enquired.

'He's just turned seventeen while in custody, my lord.'

'So he went to Lewes prison at sixteen?' He seemed as mystified as everyone else. 'Why was that?'

'We were unable to find a bail hostel for him, my lord.'

'I object to bail,' the CPS lawyer interrupted. 'Mr Peters is a high-risk individual.'

'We don't feel we should send him back to Lewes,' my QC argued on. 'Special rules were made for him by the governor because of his youth, but we don't feel we can ask for that again.'

'Well, we need to set a trial date for this,' the judge said, and I was sent back down to the cells to wait while they sorted everything out.

My QC came down a while later to assure me they were doing everything they could to get me out. I couldn't wait to be free again. He came back a couple of hours later, looking glum.

'Bad news, I'm afraid,' he said. 'We've got to go back up to the courtroom and we'll explain to you what's happening.'

It seemed that the same thing had happened again. They couldn't find a bail hostel with any room for me and so I was going to have to go back to Lewes prison.

'We can't just let you go roaming the streets,' the judge said, 'and we can't find anywhere else. I understand that the prison governor has severe reservations about you being there, but I don't see any alternative at the moment. We will mark your case as urgent, so that you are there for as short a time as possible.'

The screws couldn't believe it when I turned up again at the gates of Lewes.

'Not you again!' they said, looking genuinely shocked. 'What are you doing back here?'

'They couldn't find me anywhere to go, could they?'

'The governor's not going to be happy about this,' Matt said, shaking his head.

'Can I get back to my wing?'

'Hang on a second. Let's have those clothes back that we lent you.'

Once I was back in my uniform they took me through the first set of bars and I could see Frank playing pool through the next set.

'Oi,' I shouted, 'Frankie! I'm back.'

He froze without even turning round. Seeing him made me a bit tearful. Despite all my outward swagger and noise, he took me back under his wing with a sort of gruff kindness.

I was set to return to court during the first week in June, which meant another two months in prison. The time looked as if it stretched ahead for ever. The other prisoners had all seen through my bravado by that stage and treated me well, often sharing their sweets with me when they didn't have to, as if I was just another kid. Now that I was less afraid of the other prisoners, the biggest problems were boredom and missing Lisa. I thought about her all the time, wondering where she had been taken to and whether she was missing me as much as I was missing her. I tried to find out where she was so that I could write to her, but no one was able to give me an address.

Frank did his best to entertain both of us during the endless days we spent together. He would tell me jokes and we used to pass hours in the cell playing 'I spy with my little eye', but he would cheat, naming things that weren't even in the cell, teasing me and making me angry.

The one useful thing that came out of my boredom was that I had the opportunity to learn to read and write better. I wasn't completely illiterate at the start but I had been at school for such a short time I had never really caught up with other kids of my age. Creative reading and writing classes were a good alternative to being banged up in the cell all day and I actually found that I enjoyed writing little poems and expressing myself in ways I had never thought I could.

I continued to have sessions talking to Matt and he tried to get more out of me about what had happened at home and in Uncle Douglas's house. And a prison probation officer came in to talk to me in order to prepare pre-sentencing reports for the judge to read at the end of my trial, but I had said more than I was comfortable with already and didn't want to talk about my past any more, or go into any more detail. In the end I was quite nasty to both of them, telling them to 'mind their own business' in an attempt to shut them up so that I could get on with my life. I was fed up with looking back all the time, wallowing in self-pity.

My QC had been into the prison to see me a couple of times and had warned me that I would probably end up being sentenced to about six years for all the crimes they were taking into consideration.

'I can't do six years!' I said, horrified.

'You should have thought of that before you started on this crime spree.'

'I didn't do four hundred and sixty crimes,' I protested. 'I couldn't possibly have. I haven't even been living in the area long enough.'

'Well,' he looked doubtful, 'according to your co-defendants, Jock and Jake …'

'Co-defendants? They were the ringleaders. I just followed them.'

'Well, you did a "no comment" interview at the police station, which has gone against you because the others from the squat have all talked and cooperated with the police. They've all said you are the number one when it comes to the robberies. They've admitted to one or two minor misdemeanours, but they will probably get off with a caution because of their openness.'

Although I was furious with the others for dropping me in it, and even though the idea of serving six years or more filled me with horror, the small boy inside me couldn't help standing a bit taller at the thought that everyone seemed to think I was some sort of Mafia don. There were moments when it made me quite cocky as well as angry. If it was true that they had all said these things, it meant they hadn't even lived by their own code of sticking together and saying 'no comment'. I had been the only one who had stuck by the rules I had been set.

In the courtroom I had to stand next to the others from the house, as if we were all being tried together, when I knew they had already set me up to be the fall guy for everyone's crimes. The only one who wasn't there was Lisa, because she was still sectioned and in fact she had never been involved in any of the stealing, even though she had benefited from the results. The judge, after studying the papers, decided that because I was apparently so much worse than the rest of them I should be tried separately. I was now going to be given my own jury and, having been coached for the last few months by all the old lags in Lewes, I was pleading 'not guilty'.

On the day of my trial my QC failed to turn up and no one could find him. It didn't break my heart because I hadn't liked him or believed he was really on my side. When the court officials called his firm, they said they weren't going to be sending anyone else because they had decided not to represent me any more. I must have got up his nose just as much as he had got up mine. The prosecutor was a woman that day and the tone of her voice suggested that she could see through the brave front I was putting on and felt sorry for me.

'I'll defend myself,' I said when I was told I didn't have a lawyer any more – anything rather than be shipped back to Lewes while they started the whole process all over again.

The judge looked down at me over the top of his glasses.

'Be quiet,' he instructed.

I was taken down to the cells again while they tried to work out what to do and a while later the lady prosecutor came down to see me.

'We can't get hold of any QC to represent you,' she said. 'Is there anyone else you know?'

'I don't know anyone. He was representing me all the way through. The solicitors at the police station appointed him.'

'The judge is furious up there.' She was looking at me very thoughtfully. 'I don't think this is very fair on you, Joe. Some things have been brought to my attention …'

I realized at that moment that she must have read some of the reports Matt had done about my childhood and that was why she was being more understanding than the rest of them.

'I thought those reports were supposed to be confidential,' I said grumpily.

She ignored my protest. 'Is it true? Did all those things happen to you as a child?'

I stared down at my hands. 'Yeah.'

'Really we should talk to the police about it.'

'I don't want to talk to the police about anything. I'm in here because of the police. Why should I help them?'

She tried to gently explain how I was actually spiting myself with my attitude, and how I might be able to make my position much better by cooperating.

'Wait there a minute,' she said and when I glanced up I noticed that she seemed to have tears in her eyes. 'I'll see if I can get you a duty QC.'

When she came back she shook her head but sat down purposefully, as if she had a plan she wanted to confide in me.

'I can't find anyone who's free,' she whispered conspiratorially, 'but this is what I am going to do. I am going to drop all these charges against you apart from four. I think they've gone a bit over the top.'

'I'll be totally honest with you,' I said, 'because you're being fair to me. I did do a few of them smash and grabs.'

'Would you like to tell me which ones you did, and then I will see what I can do?'

'Will you send me back to prison if I confess?'

'No, Joe,' she said, 'I will get you out.'

I couldn't believe what I was hearing. For the first time I could remember, something was actually going my way. Someone with influence was actually offering to help me. By the time we went back upstairs she had told me she was planning to accuse me of going into the shops and taking things after someone else had done the actual breaking in.

'If you plead guilty to these charges,' she explained, 'the jury will be dismissed and you will be saving the taxpayer money, which will definitely go in your favour.'

I didn't understand much of what she was saying, but I really wanted to trust her, to put my fate in her hands and let her look after me.

'OK,' I said. 'I'll plead guilty then.'

'And would you agree to letting me represent you as defendant as well as representing the prosecution?'

I shrugged, completely unable to grasp what she was on about but knowing she was the first person to actually sound as if she might be on my side.

'If you want,' I said.

It took a while to explain to the judge what was going on, and I could tell that he found the prosecutor's suggestion shocking.

'Do you think that would really be in the interests of Mr Peters?' he enquired.

'Mr Peters is in agreement,' she said.

He seemed to see the sense in it, since no one else appeared to be willing to step forward and speak up for me. Now that we were all finally in agreement the case started to roll, with the prosecutor reading out the charges, while at the same time mentioning my terrible childhood and the fact that I had run away and was living on the streets. She already sounded more like a defence counsel than a prosecutor. She then told the judge that they had discovered that I wasn't the ringleader at all, and that the others, who had already been set free, had stitched me up. As far as I knew she was basing all this on the report that Matt had given her and the things I had said. I was shocked and touched that she believed me at a time when I still didn't trust anyone in authority. I stayed quiet and listened in amazement as she talked about how I had 'honestly' put my hand up to the four charges and how I had been anxious not to waste the court's time.

Having put the case for the prosecution, she then put her other cap on and spoke up brilliantly in my defence, talking about what an exceptionally well-behaved young man I had been in prison, which came as news to me, as I had thought I had been a complete pain to everyone who had come into contact with me.

'He has obviously learned his lesson and has had time to reflect on the error of his ways.'

I sat in silent awe and listened as she continued to make up stuff about me, which made me sound like a much nicer person than I had ever thought myself to be. Most amazingly of all, the judge seemed to be accepting everything she told him. Once she'd said all she wanted to say, he ordered a short break before sentencing, during which my champion went into the judge's chambers, no doubt to show him some of the choicer bits from Matt's and the probation officer's reports. I was no longer worried about this invasion of my privacy if it meant I didn't have to go back to Lewes.

'I think,' the judge said once I was called back up in front of him, 'that these crimes warrant a custodial sentence.' My heart sank. 'However, you have already

171

spent several months on remand. Are you sorry for what you have done?'

'Yes, sir,' I said, repressing every instinct to say something cheeky and realizing at last that someone was offering me an opportunity. 'I'm very sorry. I'm really ashamed, Your Honour.'

'As you seem sincere,' he went on, 'I will be lenient.'

He put me on probation for three years and told me to pay £400 towards court costs and £600 in compensation costs. The idea of me finding £1,000 was so completely outlandish I didn't even bother to think about it; I just concentrated on the fact that I was now going to be able to walk out of the courtroom a free man and I was not going to have to go back to the cell with old Frank. It was like a lead weight lifting off my heart.

'You are free to go,' the judge said.

It was explained to me later that they had decided to put me on probation because they thought that a probation officer would be able to offer me at least a little of the support and guidance that I should have received from my parents but which I obviously had never had. They kept me in the cells until the duty probation officer, Mr Jenkins, was able to come and meet me and bring the address of a probation hostel that I was to report to. He gave me a £10 note to make sure I had the money to get myself there.

'They're expecting you to be there by four o'clock,' he said, 'so make sure you go straight there.'

I nodded my understanding, although the moment I got out I intended to run to the outreach centre to find out what had happened to Lisa. The volunteers had always been straight with me in the past and I thought I would get more sense out of them than I would get from anyone at the hospital. The months of thinking about her and worrying about what might have happened to her after the birth were finally over, and I couldn't wait to see her and be reunited. I knew that the baby had gone now and I would never have another chance to see him, but that didn't mean that she and I couldn't get back together and support each other and maybe have another go at starting a family in a few years' time. There had been so many long, sleepless nights in the prison cell, which I had only managed to get through by imagining our future together.

Chapter Eighteen

Looking for Lisa

It felt strange to walk out of the court alone, having been escorted everywhere since the night of my arrest nearly five months before. I half expected to feel a hand on my arm at any moment and find someone was telling me there had been a mistake and I wasn't to go free after all. For months I had been told exactly what to do every moment of the day, but now there was no van or car waiting to swallow me up, just an address written on a slip of paper that I had to find my own way to.

I was taking a deep breath of fresh air and savouring the moment when I saw Ben, Jock and Jake and the others coming towards me. For a second I was pleased to see them; then I saw that they looked angry and determined, as if they had a mission and it wasn't to give me a welcome-home hug. They must have heard I was coming out and decided to come looking for me, but I wasn't sure why they were looking so angry. I waited for them to get to me so that I could tell them everything that had happened to me, confident they would be pleased that I had never given anything away, and that I had taken the fall for them just as it had always been agreed and given a 'no comment' interview.

They didn't give me a chance to say more than a couple of words before starting to lay into me, shouting about how I had 'grassed them all up' and that they had lost their home because of me. Realizing they were too drunk and riled up to listen to reason, I just wanted to get past them and run to the outreach centre to find out where Lisa was. If these people who I had assumed were my friends had all turned against me, she was my only hope. They wouldn't be daring to lay into me like this if she had been there to give them a piece of her mind. I fought as hard as I could, but the sheer weight of their numbers knocked me off my feet and their fists and feet rained down on me.

'Oi! Police,' a strong voice shouted and my attackers all scattered, leaving me on the ground as an out-of-uniform policeman jogged over to help me, flashing his badge.

'We'll radio this in and report it,' he said as he helped me up.

'I don't want you radioing in anything,' I said. 'I just want to go.'

'Don't you want to report them for that attack?'

'I don't want to report anyone. I've had enough of coppers and courts.'

'OK,' he said, holding up his hands and backing off. 'Only trying to help.'

He watched with a puzzled expression as I stumbled away before he could say anything else, diving off the main road into the back streets where I was less likely to be spotted, and making my way to the centre and to Lisa as quickly as I could. I burst in through the doors, knowing I would be safe as soon as I was inside. When the staff saw me, they all rushed over and gave me a cuddle, bombarding me with questions about everything that had happened since they last saw me. Relieved to be safe and enjoying being the centre of attention, I sat down and explained everything to them. I played them some of the police tape, which I had been carrying around in my bag, where I had said 'no comment' all the way through as Ben and Jock had taught me.

'I want to know where Lisa is,' I said when the initial excitement had died down.

They exchanged uncomfortable looks.

'We tried to ask the prison to let you out for your baby's funeral,' someone said, 'but they just wouldn't do it.'

'Where's Lisa?' I asked, feeling they were avoiding answering. 'I need to speak to her. I need to see her.'

'She was sectioned.'

'I know that. What hospital is she at now?'

'She's not in the south any more. She's gone back to her relatives up north.'

'Can I have an address or a number for her?' I asked. 'Or for these relatives?'

'We're sorry,' they said. 'They specifically instructed us not to pass on any details.'

'Not even to me?' I asked, feeling as if someone had just kicked me in the teeth.

'Not even to you. We're so sorry. Lisa wants to make a new start.'

'We were going to make a new start together,' I protested, trying to make them understand. 'In Penzance.'

I couldn't understand why they were being so evasive when all I wanted was straight answers. I felt all the frustrations and the miseries and injustices of the previous months boiling back up again. I jumped up, shouting and punching the door, unable to sit down calmly for a moment longer.

'Where is my son buried?' I screamed. 'I want to know where he is!'

'They had him cremated,' one of the key workers said.

I've never been able to get my head round the concept of cremation. It seems too final for me to cope with. I thought there should be somewhere where that perfect little body I had helped to create could lie. Somewhere that I could visit. Seeing where his ashes were was likely to bring me little comfort. I remembered the arguments that went on after my father died and how my mother insisted on having his remains cremated, even though it was well known that it would be against his wishes. Now it had happened again: other people had been making decisions about the most important things in my life, taking the people who were most precious away from me and leaving me on my own at the mercy of other people who seemed to hate me and want to hurt me.

Charlotte had finished with Jock, but was still hanging around the centre and didn't seem to share the others' anger with me. She believed me when I said I hadn't grassed anyone up and agreed to come with me to visit the ashes at the crematorium. When we got there, I realized there was nothing there for me to look at and I felt as if I had lost him all over again. He had gone and I had never had a chance to say goodbye. I felt I had been cheated. I felt there was nothing left for me to hold on to. I had imagined Lisa and I were going to be there for one another, supporting each other through the pain of our loss, but I could see now that wasn't going to happen.

When we got back to the centre, the others were there again and wanting to go back to where they had left off giving me a kicking when the policeman interrupted them. They were even drunker and shouting at the key workers to send me outside because they were going to kill me. I was so angry at the whole world by then I felt ready to take them all on, even though I wouldn't have stood a chance, not caring about the consequences.

The key worker who had listened to my police interview tape tried to convince them that they had got it all wrong, that I wasn't the one who had grassed anyone up and that it had been Jake who had told the police everything.

'I don't believe you,' Ben said, although his face told a different story as it dawned on him that he might have been lied to.

'All through his interview he stuck to saying "no comment",' the key worker insisted, 'just like you told him to.'

'Give him the bloody tape,' I said to Charlotte, fishing in my bag and handing it over. 'And tell him to keep it.'

Ben agreed to come into the centre to listen, while Jock and Jake mysteriously disappeared. He listened to nearly the whole thing, convinced for a long time that he was going to come across a bit where I had grassed, but he never found it.

'I'm happy,' he said eventually. 'I'm really sorry, Joe. You've been stitched up and I believed Jock and Jake. I'll tell the rest of them that it wasn't you and I'm sorry for giving you a belting earlier.'

I just shrugged, because there was nothing else to say. It seemed this was just the way my life was always going to be. I was tired and I wanted to sleep, so I fished out the address of the hostel that the duty probation officer had given me. By the time I got there it was dark and way past the time I was meant to report in.

'Why are you so late?' the grumpy-looking warden asked as I handed over my slip. 'Where have you been?'

'I had a few things I had to sort out,' I snapped, not in the mood to be told off by anyone else. 'What's it fucking got to do with you anyway?'

'There's no need for that. I won't tolerate that sort of language here.'

'Just show me to my room and I'll stay out of your way.'

Although I was relieved to be out of prison, I was broken-hearted to find that Lisa hadn't wanted to stay in touch with me. The shabbiness and stale stink of the halfway house, with cigarette burns in the furniture and worn lino on the floors, did nothing to rescue my plunging spirits. I was shown to my dormitory and I felt cold and empty inside as I sat on a bed in a flimsy cubicle. I just wanted to get away from the area and all the treacherous people I had got involved with – people I had foolishly thought were my friends but I now realized didn't care for me in the least. I could see clearly now that all my plans of spending my life with Lisa had just been the dreams of a foolish young boy. I knew I was going to have to move on and start all over again, but I felt totally lost and unable to work out what direction I should be heading in.

I had come to London because I'd heard other people talking about it as a sort of promised land; I had known no more about it than that. The same was true of Penzance. Lisa hadn't been the only one to tell me that it was a cool place for homeless people to go to and make fresh starts. Not having anywhere else to go to, or anyone else to ask, I decided I would take myself off there anyway, even though I would now be travelling alone and not as part of a happy little family as I had been imagining just a few months before. If I'm honest, there was a part of me that still dreamed that maybe Lisa would find her way there too and we would bump into each other, rekindle our feelings for one another and pick up where we had left off.

The next day I remained lost in thought. Other inmates at the hostel tried to make conversation, but I wanted to be left alone with my plans. I'd had enough of being forced to be with people all day long when I was in prison; now I wanted to guard what little private space I might have left in the world.

I went back to the outreach centre again, since the key workers there were the only people I had left and I still hoped that if I pleaded with them they would give me some clue as to where to find Lisa. I took my bag with me, carrying all my worldly possessions around as usual, not wanting to leave anything at the hostel and hoping I wouldn't have to go back there again. Of course they hadn't changed their minds and steadfastly refused to tell me any more.

Charlotte told me that Ben and Jock had fallen out now that Ben knew the truth, and Jake and Jock started on me again as soon as I walked into the centre, which got them chucked out and confirmed in my mind that I had to get away from the area, because they would never ultimately leave me alone. I realized now that everything to do with Jake had led me into trouble, and Jock wasn't much better.

I told the key workers that I wanted to go to Penzance and they agreed that it was a good idea. I think they were probably quite pleased to think I would then be someone else's problem. They bought me a train ticket the same day so that I didn't even have to go back to the hostel that night, plus some lunch and a bit of spending money.

'Have you informed the probation office of your plans?' they asked.

'Oh yeah,' I lied breezily. 'It's not a problem.'

I had no intention of telling anyone in case they said I couldn't go. I'd had enough in my life of being told what I could and couldn't do by other people.

I felt miserable and alone as I headed for the station with my bag over my shoulder once more and no idea what lay in store. I knew I was breaking the rules of my probation, but I was past caring. I was becoming more and more convinced that life wasn't worth living and was never going to get any better for me. All I had wanted was to be with someone I loved and who loved me. I kept on thinking about Dad, just as I had all my life, and now I found my thoughts straying to Lisa and my son as well. It didn't seem as if the pain was ever going to stop.

Chapter Nineteen

On the Beach

I had no idea how far it was to Cornwall until I had already been travelling for several hours and was changing trains for the second time at Exeter. Everyone else I came across on the journey seemed to be in high spirits, most of them heading off on their holidays, travelling with friends and families. The further west we travelled the higher I found my own spirits rising too. I still hoped in my heart that I would bump into Lisa once I arrived and that she would realize she couldn't live without me, but if that didn't happen then perhaps Cornwall would be the place where I would meet someone else, fall in love and finally live happily ever after. No matter how dark my depressions were, there were still these little outbreaks of optimism to keep me going.

I'm not sure what I expected to find when I got there, but it wasn't the bleak-looking town that greeted my eyes as we drew in at the long platform stretching alongside the main road in Penzance. I hadn't realized that the town was primarily a fishing port rather than a beach resort. I guess I had imagined walking straight into a community of people in the same position as me, just as I had imagined when I arrived at Charing Cross, but I couldn't see any homeless people anywhere. Everyone I overheard talking had strange accents that reminded me how far I was now from where I had started life. As I walked out of the station, there was a steep hill in one direction and a choppy-looking grey sea in the other.

'Is that it?' I wondered, all the high spirits and optimism that had risen inside me on the journey seeping away once more, leaving me feeling lost and alone.

It was already getting late and I didn't want to have to deal with any other officious people like hostel managers just yet with all their questions and recriminations. I wanted to get my bearings and find my feet before letting the authorities back into my life. I knew the probation services were going to be angry about me not letting them know I was moving town and I didn't want to be put back on the next train before I had even had a chance to explore.

Despite the fact that it was already growing cold and dark, I felt drawn towards the rhythmic sound of the waves on the shore, finding it strangely calming. As I got closer, the sound drowned out every other noise, making it feel as if the rest of the world was disappearing behind me, taking all its problems with it. I walked down on to the beach and began to search for a sheltered corner where I might be able to get out of the wind and perhaps eventually sleep for a few hours. I had a sleeping bag that the workers at the centre had given me and I still had some of my provisions left in my bag, so I knew I would be OK for a few nights. I walked along the promenade to an area of rocks where people went to fish before I settled myself down, huddling out of the wind, listening to the sea and counting the stars in the sky above.

It felt good to be close to nature instead of hemmed in by walls and behind boarded or barred windows. The air was fresh and salty as well as cold. Since going to creative reading and writing classes in prison I had taken to carrying a little notebook around with me, scribbling down poems that expressed how I was feeling and what I was thinking. I pulled the book out now and tried to express what I was feeling in words.

'Hello.' A surprised woman's voice penetrated the roar of the waves, interrupting my thoughts. 'I didn't see you there.'

I looked up and saw a girl in a waitress's uniform looking down at me. It was unusual for someone to start up a conversation like this, especially a young woman on her own. I immediately warmed to her just because she'd had the nerve to stop and speak to me in such a friendly way.

'Are you homeless?' she asked.

'Yeah.'

'Can I join you?'

I shrugged and she sat down bedside me, staring out at the dark sea as well. 'I like coming down here after work. It clears my head.'

'Do you live here then?' I asked. It was nice to have some company, especially someone who didn't seem to have any agenda of her own.

'I come down for the seasonal work in the hotels,' she explained. 'There must be somewhere you can go on a night like this, just to get out of the cold.'

'I'm new to Penzance,' I said. 'I'd rather stay here. I like the sea.'

She seemed to accept this response as perfectly normal and we chatted for a bit. When she got up to go on her way, she gave me some money. It was only about £15, but that would have been a lot for someone working as a waitress and I hadn't asked her for anything.

'I'll come back and see you again,' she said. 'I've got a friend called Gareth. I'll tell him about you and maybe he will have some ideas where you can go.'

'OK then.'

Once she had gone, I suddenly felt very alone and it took a while for me to settle down again on my own, eventually drifting into a fitful sleep. When I woke, I still didn't feel ready to face the authorities and decided to explore a bit first and savour my newly won freedom.

For the next two days I wandered around town a bit, trying to get my bearings, living off the last of the money that I'd been given by the workers at the centre. I went back down to the beach each night to the same place, hoping the same girl would come by again for another chat. I missed having people to talk to. Although being locked in a cell had been a nightmare, at least I'd had company. The only other homeless people I came across as I wandered around were old winos. There didn't seem to be any young people at all and at night the streets became completely deserted – nothing like the buzzing Charing Cross night scenes.

On the third evening, I'd been in my sleeping bag a few hours when a chap appeared beside me out of the gloom. I was instantly on my guard, ready to fight back to protect myself and my bag if necessary.

'Hi,' he said, his friendly tone immediately putting me at ease. 'I'm Gareth. I heard you were here but I couldn't find you last night.'

He looked, as far as I could see, as if he was in his late twenties and just as easy-going and natural as the girl had been, as if it was the most normal thing in the world to talk to a strange young homeless boy on the beach. He sat with me for a while and just chatted, telling me about how he was into bodybuilding. Even in the dim light of the moon I could see that he was pretty pumped up. (I later found out that his appearance was partly due to the large quantities of steroids he took.)

'You can't stay here for ever,' he said after a while, shivering as he spoke. 'It's too cold.'

'I'm OK,' I assured him, although I obviously wasn't. I still didn't feel ready to go into some tatty hostel and have to answer questions and obey a load of stupid rules.

'I've got a spare room,' he said. 'Why don't you have that?'

Although I was still nervous about going home with anyone I didn't know after my bad experience with Max, he seemed a genuinely nice guy and I was a bit fed up with feeling cold, so I agreed. I remembered how kind Mohamed had been to me the night I ran away and I knew that I had to start trusting people again sooner or later. We packed my stuff up and headed into town.

He had a nice basement flat, warm and secure-feeling, and we sat around talking till about seven in the morning before finally falling asleep. He told me that he worked in a pub and didn't have to go in till the afternoon. I confessed that I was on probation and explained how Jake and the others had stitched me up. I'm not sure if he believed that I had already been to prison at my age until he had heard the whole story. It actually sounded quite shocking to me when I heard myself telling it. I don't think he thought I was seventeen either at first; people still never seemed to believe I was as old as I was.

'You'd better go and see the probation officer down here,' he said, 'because you don't want to get on the wrong side of them.'

I knew he was right. Although I had no plans to get into trouble, if a policeman were to pick me up for something or other I would be in twice as much bother. I felt better about handing myself in now that I had a friend in the town. Gareth gave me a key to the flat so that I could come and go as I pleased, and so that I would be able to tell the authorities I had somewhere to stay. The next afternoon, once he'd gone to work, I walked into the probation office with my heart crashing in my ears and briefly explained the situation to the receptionist. She then fetched a probation officer, called Carol, who sat me down and listened patiently to the whole story.

'You realize you've breached your bail conditions, don't you?' she said.

'Yeah,' I said, 'I know. But I felt I was in danger there. They were going to beat me up again if they got a chance.'

'But you've made yourself homeless.'

'No, I haven't. I've got somewhere to stay here. I've got a friend with a flat. He's given me a key.' I held it up proudly. 'If you ring the outreach centre where I've come from they'll tell you all about me. They'll tell you that they agreed I should come.'

Carol went out of the office to make the phone call, leaving me fidgeting nervously in my seat.

'They seem to think you told your probation officer you were coming here,' she said as she came back in.

'Not quite,' I admitted. 'That's why I've come to tell you.'

'Oh dear,' she said, sitting back down. 'Well, you're here now, so you might as well stay. I'd better send for your papers. You must report to me every week, Joe, and not go off again without telling me. OK?'

'Yes,' I said, as innocently as I could manage. 'OK.'

I meant it too, because I could sense that she actually was keen to help me in any way she could and I realized I was going to need all the help I could get if I wanted to improve my lot in life.

The first problem was how I was going to support myself. Because I was still under eighteen I couldn't get dole money and she agreed to help me find out how I could get assistance, as long as I agreed to go to college and try to get some sort of skill or qualification. I didn't object to any of this. I was very happy to work and make something of myself if someone would just show me where to get started. I certainly didn't want to sit around doing nothing all my life, ending up like the old winos I'd met in London. But Carol was going a bit fast for me. She was asking me questions about 'careers' and what it was that I wanted from life, when I was still at the stage of wondering how I would survive each day and where I would be sleeping each night.

To keep her quiet I told her that I fancied working with animals, and to be honest I did think that it would be better than having to deal with people all day, since other people had been the cause of every problem I had ever had. She decided that she would find a way of getting me into farming, which sounded fine to me.

While she set about organizing that, I went back to the flat and Gareth started to introduce me to other friends around the town. We spent a lot of time hanging out together and one day the two of us were walking down a road called Belmont Terrace when we heard giggling and wolf whistling coming from above. Looking up, we saw some girls leaning out of an upstairs window, trying to attract our attention.

'Hi,' Gareth said, laughing, and I could tell he knew them already. 'Where's your mum? Where's Sue?'

The girls shouted over their shoulders for their mother until she appeared at the window too and it was obvious that Gareth fancied her, even though she must have been at least ten years older than him.

'Can we come up for a cuppa?' Gareth asked.

'Yeah, come up.' They were laughing and joking as we waited downstairs to be let in.

They lived in the top-floor flat of a massive Victorian house and seemed like the happiest, most welcoming bunch of people I had ever met. Sue, I soon discovered, had three daughters and a son. Two of the girls, Kirsty and Tammy, were from her first marriage, and Sam and Lee were from her second marriage. She had divorced for a second time and was living on her own in the house with the kids. They were bantering and flirting away and I was having trouble keeping my eyes off Kirsty, who I thought was really pretty.

I tried not to blush or stutter and they asked me all sorts of questions about who I was and where I had come from, seeming to be genuinely interested in my answers, although I only said that I'd had a rough time and had run away to Cornwall to escape. I was tired of talking about my past and I thought it made me sound more mysterious and romantic if I didn't say too much. It felt as if they had become my friends the moment we walked through their door, and Tammy seemed to adopt me as if I was a new little brother, as if I was already part of the family.

We started going down to the pub together in the evenings and they were just a beautiful, loving little family. I couldn't believe how supportive Sue was of her children, compared to how my mother had been towards all of us and me in particular. She seemed to instantly include me as one of them and the more time I spent with them the further in love with Kirsty I fell. Could this be the love of my life that I had been searching for? I wondered. She was certainly very different from Lisa, and had the added attraction of being surrounded by a ready-made happy family. Whereas Lisa and I had been like two lonely survivors clinging together for protection against a hostile world and cruel fates, Kirsty and her family were like a safe port that I could sail into for sanctuary.

Chapter Twenty

Farmer Joe

At the same time as I was settling into my new social life in Penzance, Carol, my probation officer, was working away at getting me on to a college course, despite the fact that I had no education and a track record of being a bit of a handful. She was obviously not one to be easily discouraged and within a couple of weeks she had got me enrolled in a college in St Austell, which was a fair distance away.

'We'll have to find you some accommodation there,' she said. 'You wouldn't be able to travel back and forth every day. It's too far.'

Although I was grateful to her for caring enough to make the effort, I really didn't want to leave Penzance and my new-found family and friends; nor did I want to have to change to yet another probation officer and have to explain myself all over again to someone new. I didn't want to go back to being lonely when I had just found a place where I could feel that I belonged. Carol, however, wasn't going to let me put her off and sent me to visit the college she had found and to meet the man who had agreed to be my tutor.

He was a funny little man who spent the whole time stroking his ginger moustache as he talked. He obviously knew I was in trouble because I was on probation, but he still seemed willing to give me a chance. I think the course they were offering me was partly funded by the Prince's Trust, which is set up to help kids like me get a start in life. Most of the course, he explained, would involve work placement on an actual farm.

'Can I go to a farm somewhere near Penzance for the work experience?' I asked. 'Because that's where I have friends.'

He said he would see what he could do, which I thought was pretty decent of him under the circumstances, and a few days later he came back to Carol and told her that he had found a farmer at Zennor, a village between the towns of St Just and St Ives, who was willing to take me on and give me a chance. The farm was only about an hour's walk from Penzance and meant that Carol could continue being my probation officer.

Then I heard that Sue and her family were being offered a council house in St Just, which seemed like a sign that things were meant to be. Something was finally going right for me. The farmer I was going to be working for at Zennor was a widowed lady who had been left with a farm which was too much for her to manage on her own. It was a live-in position with food provided and she was a really nice woman. I was to live with her in the old farmhouse, which had an Aga and all the traditional country comforts.

My duties covered just about every aspect of farm life. I had to feed the chickens and the pigs, and milk the cows. I would also go to college a couple of days a week to learn all about agriculture. The old lady showed me how to do everything; she even taught me how to drive the tractor, which I loved doing. I took it out on the road sometimes, although I don't think I was strictly supposed to, feeling very free and grown-up, as if I was finally getting a grip on my life and amounting to something worthwhile. I worked hard from six every morning to six in the evening and it felt good because I was learning so much. I far preferred it to drifting around the streets of some city all day, or hanging around in a squat or a basement, drinking and smoking and talking rubbish with a bunch of drunks.

At the end of each week I had £35 in my pocket, which seemed like a fortune to me, since all my living costs were taken care of. I even bought myself a pushbike so that I could get around faster.

I met a lovely girl called Holly, who was from a posh local family and who I fancied almost as much as I fancied Kirsty. I soon realized that neither of them were interested in being anything other than my friend, which was a disappointment and reaffirmed my suspicion that I was ultimately unlovable and was going to have to resign myself to ending up alone. Although it was wonderful to have a circle of friends who felt almost like family, what I still wanted more than anything else was a soulmate, someone who would be just for me in the way Lisa had been. I tried everything to win Kirsty over, and her sister Tammy used to take the mickey out of me something terrible as a result.

Quite soon after I met them I thought it would be a good idea to take Kirsty a little bouquet as a token of my love. I had no money at all at that stage, so I borrowed some flowers from the local graveyard on my way over. That was bad enough, but I also forgot to take the 'with sympathy' card out.

I could see that Kirsty was very touched when I first handed them over, even if Tammy was already mocking me over her sister's shoulder. Then she found the card.

'Oh my God, Joe,' she yelled, 'you've nicked these off someone's grave.'

The whole family fell about laughing as my face turned the colour of beetroot. None of them was ever going to let me forget that.

Every weekend I was free to please myself and I would always walk into St Just to see the others, drawn to them like a magnet. One Saturday they told me they were going to be throwing a barbecue and I thought I had better make a contribution by taking something with me. They were always doing things for me and I was finally in a position to give something back. I thought I would ask the farmer if I could take some chops because I knew she had freezers full of different cuts of meat which she held back from the butcher.

The day of the party she had gone out and I thought I would help myself to something and then offer to pay her from my wages later. Before setting out for St Just, I went to the main deep freeze and rummaged around amongst the various bags and boxes for the right thing. It was hard to see because all the plastic wrappings were frosted up, but I eventually came across a bag which seemed about the right size for a big family party. I could just see through one side of the plastic and it looked like nice meat, so I decided on that one and closed the lid. I felt a bit bad about doing it without asking the farmer's permission, but she had always been so nice to me I thought it would be OK. I popped it into a carrier bag and cycled over to St Just.

There were already lots of their friends and family at the house and the barbecue was blazing away by the time I got there. They all gave me my usual warm welcome and introduced me to anyone I didn't already know.

'Look at that for a chop,' I said proudly as I handed Sue the carrier bag, which she took through into the kitchen to unpack. I think she was a bit shocked by the size of it, but grateful for the meat none the less. I was just getting myself a drink and chatting to everyone when I heard screams coming from inside the house.

Everyone was running in to see what was going on. The women in the kitchen were screaming and laughing and running around, apparently not knowing what to do.

'What the fuck is that?' someone said and I looked across at the table, where my bag was now open, revealing half a defrosting pig's head, complete with eye and ear and teeth.

'Get it out of my kitchen!' Sue was screaming while everyone else was falling about laughing.

Although I was embarrassed for a moment at having made such a mistake, I became the centre of the party from then on, forever known as the man who had brought the pig's head to a family barbecue – on top of being the man who had nicked the flowers from the graveyard – and I enjoyed the feeling of being a part of this good-humoured family's folklore. I liked it when they all took the mickey, because it always felt as if they were doing it with affection.

The next day at the farm I should have mentioned it to the farmer and offered to pay her for it, but I think I was a bit embarrassed at having made such a gauche mistake and I wasn't sure how to bring the subject up. Whatever the reason, I missed my opportunity and then a couple of days had gone past and it seemed too late to say anything. As I got on with my job, I gradually forgot about the incident until the day that she asked if she could have a word.

'Of course,' I said. I always liked talking to her because I usually ended up learning something new.

'Someone has been taking things from my deep freeze and I just wondered if you know anything about it.'

I felt sick inside and instantly realized I had made a mistake.

'I actually took half a pig's head,' I confessed. 'I'm very sorry. I should have told you.'

'What would you have done with half a pig's head?' she asked, looking completely baffled.

'I took it to a barbecue,' I said, expecting her to laugh at my stupidity as the others had.

She looked at me with her mouth hanging open. 'Oh,' she said, recovering herself. 'I'm not very happy with that, Joe. You should have asked me first.'

There was nothing I could say to that. I immediately offered to pay her back out of my wages but I could see that with that one stupid mistake I had lost her trust and made her question the wisdom of keeping me around. Even though it seemed a relatively trivial thing, I had acted dishonestly and I could see that she was uncomfortable having me coming and going from her house after that. She also reported the incident to my gingermoustached tutor at the college and said that she didn't want to have me on the farm any more. I was very sad that the incident seemed to be getting blown out of proportion because I had liked working there, but in the end I knew it was my own stupid fault.

Everyone was disappointed in me and Carol said that I would have to move to St Austell now to finish the course, but I was still adamant I didn't want to start again with another probation officer. I know I was being quite stubborn and difficult about it, but I was learning that if I didn't stick up for myself no one else was going to do it for me.

'All right,' Carol said eventually, and I could see she was trying really hard to find a solution I would be happy with. 'I will come and visit you on your next placement, wherever that might be.'

I really appreciated that gesture because she didn't have to make it and it might cause her a lot of inconvenience if I was placed somewhere a long way from Penzance. The college found me another placement on a farm where they bred and trained horses and kept pigs. The owner said that if it worked out they would teach me how to ride and jump and all sorts of other exciting things.

'They'll teach you a lot here,' my tutor said before dropping me off, 'so don't fuck it up.'

I was a bit wary of the horses to start with, but as I got more used to being around them and grooming them I started to really enjoy the work. My relationship with the family, however, did not go so well. These people were quite posh and so I wasn't allowed in their house, having to live all the time in a cold caravan in one of the fields; and their daughter, who was about my age, didn't take to me at all and made sure I knew it. Despite all their promises, they never allowed me to get on a horse, just making me clean out the stables and the pigsties all day long. I tried my hardest to be nice because I really didn't want to let Carol and my tutor down again, but they were horrible to me and I became more and more miserable sitting alone in my caravan in the evenings, staring out the window at the pitch black of the countryside. They didn't teach me anything new as they had promised and as the lady before had done.

What I had also not realized was that my tutor had conveniently forgotten to tell them that I had been in trouble. To be honest, they probably wouldn't have agreed to take me on if he had mentioned it. So when Carol turned up for a visit and they realized I was on probation, they kicked up a right stink.

'We don't want him here,' they told her, 'if he's a criminal.'

'They're only using me to shift pig shit anyway,' I muttered. 'I've learned nothing.'

'Oh!' The mistress of the house looked as if she was about to faint. 'You are so ungrateful.'

'You'd better pack your bags, Joe,' Carol said sadly, able to see that things were not likely to work out there.

I could see the horror on my tutor's face the next day when we walked back into his office.

'It was your fault this time, Ginge,' I said before he could start having a go.

'Why?' he protested. 'What have I done?'

'You forgot to mention to them that he was on probation,' Carol said.

'Ah,' he said, reddening. 'It must have slipped my mind.'

We sat in his office and waited as he rang round everywhere he could think of, but no one had a place for me. I could see he was close to giving up. It was getting dark outside when he finally hung up from a call, looking triumphant.

'Right,' he said, 'I've called in a good favour off a chap called Andy. I owe this man a lot, so don't let me down. He runs an equestrian centre called St Leonards near Launceston. He's going to come over and collect you now.'

When Andy showed up, I was struck by how gently spoken he was and immediately warmed to him. I wanted to make sure he knew all about me so that he wouldn't be able to say we had lied to him later.

'Let's not worry about anything in the past,' he said when I explained I was on probation. 'I'm not interested. We're going to start afresh from today. Don't worry about it at all, kid. Come and meet us and see what you think. I promise you'll learn a lot if you decide to stay.'

Although I liked him, I still wasn't going to get my hopes up too soon. I'd heard these sorts of promises before, but I knew from the way the farmer in St Just had treated me that there were good people out there who were willing to give me the benefit of the doubt, so I said nothing and went with him.

'I've sorted out a guesthouse for you to stay in,' he told me as we drove back together. 'They're friends of mine, so you'll be OK. I'll drop you off there now and come and collect you in the morning, and we'll show you the ropes. We'll have some fun.'

By the time we got to the guesthouse, which was really nice, I was feeling as if I had known Andy all my life and I was looking forward to seeing his place the next day. I think he'd taken on a lot of troubled kids in the past and he knew exactly how to handle me. His partner ran the shop side of the business, selling tack and feed and everything else a rider or horse owner might need. The place was always buzzing and busy. All he asked was that I did a good job of whatever he asked me to do, and he would be happy. He was firm but always fair. He handed me over to his stable girl, who was called Claire. She showed me around and introduced me to all the horses, including a stallion that was a complete psycho.

'Whatever you do, don't turn your back on him,' she warned, 'or he'll take a chunk out of you.'

The one I liked the best was an old shire horse called Benjamin. He was nearly nineteen hands high. By the end of the first day I had already learned how to put a bridle on a horse, and it wasn't long before I could saddle up and ride the horses myself, progressing all the way up to galloping. It was the most fantastic feeling to be crashing across the open fields with the wind in my face, feeling so fast and powerful and in control. Claire and I used to take groups out riding virtually every day and I loved every minute of it.

Andy was more than as good as his word about teaching me things and allowing me to have some fun at the same time, and I know there are a lot of other boys like me who owe him more than they can ever repay. People like him don't get enough credit for the good they do in the world and the difference they make to people's lives. He showed me so much trust and taught me so much. He built my self-confidence and made me believe that maybe the world wasn't such a terrible place to live in after all, and that there were some good people out there who wanted to help me rather than abuse me. He was the closest thing to a father that I'd had since the day Dad died, even more than Frank and Matt had been in Lewes prison.

Although I was totally happy there, I decided after a year that it was time to move on and take my new-found self-confidence out into the wider world. I suppose it was a bit like growing up and leaving home again, only this time I was doing it properly rather than running away as I had when I was fifteen. I'd finished my college course and I could have done another one, but I felt I needed to do something different. It was a hard decision and Andy tried to persuade me to stay, but I think he realized I wanted to see a bit more of the world.

'There'll always be a job here for you if you change your mind,' he said as he shook my hand, and even at that moment I still wasn't sure whether I was doing the right thing or not.

However good they might be to me, and however many friends I might have met in Cornwall, I knew that at the end of the day I still had to make my own way in the world. Kirsty had fallen in love with a nice guy called Gary and I knew I was never going to be anything more than a brother and a friend to her, which broke my heart a little bit. I still wanted to meet someone that I could fall in love with and who would love me back. I wanted to repeat the experience I'd had with Lisa, but this time with someone who would stick with me through the bad times as well as the good, and I didn't think I was going to meet anyone as long as I stayed in one place, especially working on a farm in the middle of the countryside. Because I had been behaving myself and getting glowing reports from Andy, the courts had agreed to discharge my probation order early. Even my ginger college tutor was happy with me. I went back to St Just and Penzance for a while to see Sue and Gareth and the rest of the family for a couple of weeks before setting off back out into the world.

My whole life was like one long mission to find love. Where, I wondered as I packed my faithful old bag yet again, should I go from here?

Chapter Twenty-One

A Walk on the Wild Side

I decided to try living in Plymouth, just up the coast in Devon. After so long on the farms I fancied the idea of going back to a city, and I also fancied being beside the sea again. A few people had told me it was a nice place and it didn't seem too far from the family in Cornwall if I felt I needed to go back. I was in a better position than I had been when I first arrived in the other cities, because I had been able to save up a bit of money while I was working for Andy, so I booked myself into a guesthouse for the first night rather than sleeping rough as I had in the past. It felt like progress and made me think I stood a better chance of making a life for myself here.

I was exploring the streets on my own the next day, just as I had done in London and Penzance, when I met Colin, another Scottish guy like Jock, who seemed eager to chat and be friendly. He was a year younger than me and seemed to know the city well and have a lot of time on his hands.

'I'm looking for somewhere to rent,' I told him.

'You can share with me if you want,' he said. 'I've got a flat.'

His flat turned out to be in a rundown block deep in the heart of the red light district. Both the building and the area around it were full of winos and down and outs, which was fine by me, as I was more than used to such people and didn't feel threatened. The hookers were everywhere on the street outside, but they soon got to know who lived in the building and didn't bother to tout for business when they saw us, knowing we had no money, although Colin fantasized about using their services often enough. The women all looked a bit rough to me – nothing like Kirsty or Lisa or the sorts of girls that I was drawn to – but they were always very friendly and chatty.

There was one girl in particular who was often waiting for business on the pavement outside our front door and used to smile at me a lot. Colin knew her, so we got talking. She was called Trisha and lived in the block opposite ours, which was run by the council for single mums and victims of domestic violence, many of whom seemed to have been forced to go on the game in order to make ends meet. Trisha was about twenty-two and already had a baby girl called Amy to support. Colin and I used to go over to visit her sometimes and I realized that Trisha often left Amy on her own when she went out to work, and the child always seemed to be crying.

'You shouldn't do that,' I told her. 'You shouldn't leave her on her own. Anything could happen to her.'

Although I had no reason to think Trisha was mistreating Amy as Mum had mistreated me, I still didn't like the idea of Amy lying in her cot with no one coming when she cried. It reminded me too much of what I'd felt like all those years that I sobbed on my own in the cellar under Mum's house.

'I can't afford to pay babysitters,' Trisha retorted sharply, making me think that she knew it wasn't right but didn't believe she had an option. 'And I have to work to get food.'

'I'll babysit for you a few nights a week if you like,' I said, quite surprising myself with the offer.

'Would you do that for me, Joe?' she said, her whole face lighting up and making me feel pleased I'd spoken up. 'That would be brilliant.'

Whenever I was left in charge of Amy I would give her bottles and change her nappies and I found I really enjoyed doing it. Sometimes if she wasn't sleeping I would lie down on Trisha's bed and cuddle Amy until we both fell asleep, and I would imagine it was my own little baby that I was holding and caring for. Trisha would come back in the small hours sometimes and find us both fast asleep together. If it was a cold night I would just stay there, even once Trisha had come home, and go back to sleep rather than cross the road to go home. Trisha seemed to think it was really nice for a man to be interested in looking after a child and once or twice she suggested we should start a relationship. I did think she was attractive and I really liked her as a friend, but I could never have fallen for someone who was in that line of work. I always remembered how frightened I had been for those few days when I thought I might be HIV positive, and anyway my dream was to fall in love and find my soulmate, which wouldn't work if my girlfriend was selling sex to other men.

'You wouldn't want to give up working, would you?' I said when she asked if I would go out with her.

'I can't give it up,' she said. 'Some nights I can make two hundred quid. What else could I do that would earn money like that?'

I was aware that I was mixing with the wrong sort of people if I was hoping to fall in love and make something better of my life. So I got involved with the Plymouth Christian Centre and made a few friends there. I had a nagging unhappiness deep inside me all the time, however hard I worked to distract myself, and I think for a while I was hoping that I would be able to find my way to happiness and fulfilment through God, but it didn't work. I was still too angry with Him for all the things that he had allowed to happen to me when I was a kid and for the way he had taken Lisa and the baby away from me in such a cruel fashion.

I wanted to work because I had liked the feeling of earning my keep when I was with Andy, but it wasn't so easy to find a job without the help of Carol and my ginger tutor, so both Colin and I were signing on each week and the hours hung heavy most days. I found that when I had too much time to think my mind always went back to dwelling on my past, making me feel sorry for myself. We went for every job interview we were given but the moment we told prospective employers what part of town we were living in they seemed to lose interest. Under Colin's influence and without the support and stimulation of Andy, Claire, Carol and the family I went back to drinking to pass the time and kill the pain inside my head. I was smoking pot again as well, which I hadn't done since leaving the squat. It eased the depression but gradually wore away any chance I might have had when I arrived in the city of getting to grips with life.

One of the elders at the church had a brother who had an antique shop with a Christian café upstairs and I started working for him for a bit of cash, lifting stuff into the van and whatever else he needed doing. There was a joyful old Irish lady called Lulu who used to use the café a lot because it was so cheap and she always made me laugh whenever I was with her. She wasn't a Christian herself, describing the rest of them as 'bloody bible-bashers'. She had a son who was a chef and who she didn't approve of.

'He's a bad boy,' she said. 'He's into all these drugs.'

She wasn't at all happy about me living in the area where I was and kept trying to persuade me to move into her flat with her in St Jude's, which was a really nice area, but I liked being with Colin and I didn't think living with an old lady would be the right thing to do if I was hoping to meet girls.

Although I did everything I could to keep myself busy and distracted, the loneliness of not having a loving partner kept on gnawing away at my insides. I had been so happy in my relationship with Lisa and I was terrified that I would never experience that level of happiness again. One night I woke up from a nightmare, drenched in sweat. I'd been dreaming that I was a kid again, locked in a dark room with men coming and going, doing what they wanted to me. As I lay shivering in the damp bed, I felt overwhelmed with misery. It seemed I would never be able to find the sort of love and security that I craved. I couldn't bear to think about it, so I got up and poured myself a drink, swallowing it in one and pouring another straight away. Even that didn't numb the pain and I started slashing at my wrists, willing to try anything that might relieve the frustration and tension and misery building up inside my head.

As I sank deeper and deeper into depression, I began to lose my grip on everything. I turned up late for work at the antique shop one day and when the boss got cross I just told him to 'fuck off'. Although I knew he had been doing me a favour by giving me the job, he had also been using me as cheap labour and I didn't like the fact that he was now judging me. I stamped upstairs to the café and found Lulu having her lunch.

'What's the matter with you?' she wanted to know when she saw the expression on my face.

'I just had a bad night,' I told her, slumping down in the next seat.

She could see that I was down without asking any more questions and she insisted on taking me home with her that afternoon.

'You're not to go back to that terrible place,' she said. 'I've got a room here you can have.'

I soon realized that there was only one bedroom and it turned out she was offering for me to have her bed and she would sleep on the sofa in the other room. At first I absolutely refused, but she wasn't going to accept my protests. 'I always end up sleeping in the sitting room anyway,' she said, dismissing the generosity of her offer. 'It makes no difference to me.'

This time I gave in and agreed. There was something so comforting about being with her and talking to her. She had a friend called Peggy who lived opposite and the two of them had all the time in the world for me. Colin was a bit fed up that I wasn't around and accused me of neglecting my mates, but I knew Lulu was right: that I wouldn't be able to pull myself together as long as I was living in that area with him and Trisha and the rest of them. I needed a bit of time to think and work out what I should do next.

My reading and writing had got pretty good by this stage, and I had discovered that I could draw as well. I would spend hours with pencil and paper, just doodling, trying to undo the muddle of thoughts in my head. I did a portrait for Peggy, which I was very pleased with.

Part of my problem, I decided, was that I wasn't mobile. I needed to have a car. I know now that I should have taken driving lessons and got a licence first, but I didn't realize that was how it worked and I had learned the basics from driving the tractor on the farm. I saw a very old Ford Granada for sale on the side of the road for a couple of hundred pounds and I had just enough money in my pocket, so I bought it and Colin taught me a few rules of the road.

Despite all Lulu and Peggy's hard work in trying to distract me from my inner demons, I was still struggling with depression and I decided one Saturday morning to take the train back down to Cornwall to pay a visit to the family and see if that would raise my spirits. I didn't think my driving was good enough for me to take the car, and I didn't have enough money for the petrol anyway. I was still drinking much too much and for some reason I decided to get off the train at a random station before reaching Penzance, having consumed most of a bottle of vodka. There was probably no logical reason for choosing that particular stop, because nothing I did had much purpose or logic at that time; I was just drifting around in the world in a drunken fog trying to find where I was supposed to fit in, cursing God for making me so ugly and unattractive that nobody would love me, feeling sorry for myself.

Chapter Twenty-Two

Descent into Madness

I t was late at night and I remember ricocheting around the streets and eventually passing out beside a building somewhere; then there is a blank and the next thing I remember is being woken by the sound of a metal door clanging back. I opened one eye and saw a police sergeant looking down at me. With a horrible sinking feeling in my stomach, I gradually realized I was in a police cell without the faintest idea what I had done or how I had got there. I couldn't even remember what town I was in until he told me.

'What the hell am I doing here?' I moaned, clutching my throbbing head.

'Got a hangover, have we?' he teased. 'Come on, we have to book you in now. You were so pissed when you came in we couldn't do anything with you.'

I gingerly lowered my feet to the floor. I didn't want to make any fuss until I could remember what I had done and until my head had stopped hurting. Was I in big trouble? Had I put a brick through a shop window again? Or was it something even worse? Was I going to end up back in court or in prison? As I followed him meekly out of the cell, doubled up with the pain in my head, I tried in vain to force my brain to bring back the lost hours of the previous night.

'Right,' the policeman said once he was behind his desk and had his papers out in front of him. 'We're charging you with impersonating a police officer.'

'What the fuck have I done?'

I couldn't believe it. Surely I would remember doing something like that?

'You were banging on the door here, making a right row,' he said, 'demanding to be let in because you were a police officer.'

I concentrated as hard as I could but nothing he was saying rang any bells. There was still only a huge blank space in my memory between passing out in the street and waking up in the cell.

'We thought you were a trainee copper with a problem at first,' he said. 'Till we ran your prints through the system. You wasted a fair bit of our time before we realized who you really were.'

'Honest to God,' I said, 'I don't remember anything.'

Fortunately I had finally learned enough to cooperate in situations like this rather than giving them a load of cheek. They must have been able to see the funny side of it and they ended up just giving me a caution for impersonating a police officer under the influence of alcohol.

'But you're asking me to admit to something I don't even remember,' I protested weakly when they asked me to agree to it.

'It's either that or we'll have to charge you,' he said.

'Oh, all right.'

I just wanted to get back out into the fresh air and avoid having to go into any more cells. The paperwork was duly done and I was sent on my way.

The first thing I needed as I stumbled back out into the street was to find a drink to try to clear my head and stop my hands from shaking. I bought a bottle of vodka and took a deep swig, immediately feeling better. One swig was never going to be enough, though, and I took several more. Within a short time I was back to feeling numb and my head had stopped throbbing, but even the alcohol couldn't raise me out of the depression that was now gripping my insides like a vice. I felt almost physically sick with misery and loneliness.

I was walking around the town in a daze, with no idea where I was, and found myself back up at the railway lines. I stood for a moment staring at them, trying to make sense of my thoughts and to bring my eyes into focus. I didn't want to live any more and this seemed like an obvious way to put a stop to the pain. I decided I would just lie down on the track and wait for a train to come along and end it all. What was the point of going on? I was no use to anyone and no one loved me and I just kept getting into trouble. Every time something good happened to me, like Andy taking me on, I would mess it up by moving on. I was never going to find whatever it was that I was searching for and it would only be a matter of time before I found myself back in prison, and I didn't want to live a life like that.

Because it was Sunday everything was pretty quiet as I settled myself down on the track to wait for the next train.

'Oi, you!' A loud, angry voice penetrated my thoughts. 'Get off the track!'

I looked up and saw a man in uniform coming out of a signal box a few yards away. I was so wrapped up in my own thoughts I hadn't even noticed the signal box was there.

'Fuck off and leave me alone,' I slurred.

'Come on, lad, move it.'

He took a firm hold of my arm and tried to pull me off, so I took a wild swing at him with my bottle.

'Right,' he jumped back. 'I'm calling the police. This is British Rail property. You're trespassing. They'll get you off.'

I didn't care who he called because I assumed I would be dead by the time they arrived. I was too drunk to even work out that he would have changed the signals to stop any trains coming until he had got me off the track. Through the blur of vodka I saw the police coming a few minutes later. This wasn't what I wanted. This could only lead to me being locked into another cell.

'Fuck off!' I screamed at them. 'Leave me alone.'

I pulled myself groggily to my feet, smashing the now empty bottle on the line and waving the jagged end at them as a weapon in my left hand as I swayed back and forth. They immediately backed off, realizing that I was capable of causing them some serious injury if they tried to rush me.

'Don't be stupid, lad,' one of them said. 'Drop the bottle so we can talk.'

They started to move towards me, very slowly, as if they were trying to creep up on a wild animal.

'Don't come near me,' I screamed, 'or I swear I'll stab myself.'

They took no notice and took another step closer, so I plunged the broken glass into the right-hand side of my chest.

'Fuck, he's done it,' one of them shouted. I looked down and there was blood gushing everywhere, but I couldn't feel any pain. It was almost as if it was happening to someone else.

'I'll do it again if you come near me,' I said, staggering on my feet, willing myself to stay upright. I was just sober enough to know that if I intended to kill myself I had done it on the wrong side and I needed to change hands if I wanted to reach my heart. I tried to take the bottle in my right hand.

The police didn't hang back this time: they launched themselves at full speed. One of them grabbed my hand and threw me to the floor. The blood was now pumping out of me in a fountain, drenching all of us as we struggled on the ground. I could hear them shouting, but it was starting to sound as if they were a long way away.

'Get an ambulance!'

They were trying to handcuff me to stop me punching and fighting at the same time as trying to staunch the blood and keep my heart going. I was having trouble breathing, having pierced one of my lungs. I could actually hear air escaping from the hole. After a few moments of struggling to get free of the police, I slid towards unconsciousness, even though they were slapping my face to try to keep me with them until the ambulance got there. I was vaguely aware of the sound of sirens. The traffic on the railway bridge had to be stopped so that they could get as close as possible. I was aware of the paramedics coming down on to the track and trying to stop the blood, and then I let go and drifted away.

The next time I woke up I was in an unfamiliar room again, for the second time that day. I was in a bed and I was aware of machinery all around. I tried to sit up and couldn't understand why I was unable to. It took a few seconds to work out that my wrists had been strapped to the sides of the bed. I soon realized it was a hospital room, not a cell, but I was a prisoner just the same, tied up and unable to resist if anyone wanted to do anything to me. A thousand old fears came rushing to the surface, but as I tried to push against the straps and sit up, a massive wave of pain shot through my chest, knocking me back down on to the pillow gasping for breath.

When I was able to muster the strength, I looked down again and saw there was a tube going into my lung. There were stitches all round the wound in my chest and there was blood coming out into a bottle. I later discovered they were trying to drain the lung of blood so that they could re-inflate it. As I took in more of my surroundings, I realized I had a drip going into my arm and I was on a heart monitor as well. There was what looked to me like yellow dye painted on my skin. A nurse came into the room and noticed I was awake.

'Hello, sweetheart,' she said. 'Is there anything I can do for you?'

'Undo my hands, please.'

'I can't do that, darling.'

'Please,' I begged, desperate to be able to move around a little and not to feel so trapped.

'I just can't, not until we can be sure you won't do yourself any more harm. Is there anyone I can call for you, to let them know where you are?'

'No.'

There was no one to call. The only people who might have cared would have been Sue and her family, or Lulu, and I didn't want to bother any of them. I wasn't their responsibility and I didn't want any of them to see me like this. A doctor came in and introduced himself, although he didn't tell me at the time that he was a psychiatrist.

'How are you feeling mentally?' he asked.

'How the fuck do you think I'm feeling mentally?' I spat. 'I've got my hands tied and I can't move.'

'That's for your own safety. When your treatment is finished here we will be transferring you to the local psychiatric unit. You are being sectioned under the Mental Health Act for a twenty-eight day period, so that we can assess you.'

It sounded a lot like another prison sentence to me.

Once he had gone, the nurse came back in and I pleaded again for her to release my hands.

'If I do that, you have got to promise to behave,' she said, 'because if you do something to yourself I will be to blame and it will cost me my job.'

'OK,' I said, after a moment's thought. 'That's fair enough.'

She undid me and I rubbed my wrists.

'I hate those bastards,' I said, nodding towards the doctors outside. 'They're saying I'm mad. I'm not mad.'

'Darling,' she said with a sweet smile, 'you stabbed yourself with a broken bottle.'

'It was the drink,' I said, although I could see her point, 'not me.'

'Well, you won't be getting any of that in here.'

Cutting out the alcohol so suddenly was a terrible shock to my body, even with the medication they gave me to try to help, leaving me shaking and sweating and drifting in and out of consciousness over the following days. I hadn't realized how badly addicted I had become. Once I was through that, and had had the tube removed from my lung and the hole sewn up, they were ready to move me to the psychiatric hospital. Two enormous psychiatric nurses turned up to make sure I got there and didn't try to do a runner on the way. I could see they were not the sort of men that I would want to piss off and so I behaved myself and they were both really nice to me as a result. I had no idea what this place they were escorting me to was going to be like, but I didn't feel optimistic.

Chapter Twenty-Three

Bids for Freedom

The other patients in the psychiatric unit were a real mixture of ages and types. I had been expecting the worst when I heard that was where they were taking me. In fact everyone else seemed pretty friendly, and no one tried to bully me or be nasty, but from the moment I walked through the door I was trying to work out how I was going to escape.

I noticed that none of the windows opened more than a few inches and there were two sets of locked doors to get through, with two big male nurses standing guard at all times. There were high fences all round the perimeter of the grounds and cameras everywhere. I could see it was going to be a challenge.

A doctor came to check up on my wound as soon as I was admitted and he seemed quite pleased by its progress.

'Can I go then?' I asked, knowing what the answer would be.

'I'm afraid not,' he smiled. 'We need to keep you here for a while to try to work out what is wrong with you.'

'There's nothing wrong with me.'

'That is a bit debatable, isn't it, Joe? You plunged a piece of broken glass into your chest and could easily have killed yourself. And if the police hadn't stopped you, you would have done it again into your heart.' He nodded towards the scars on my wrists. 'And that's another thing we need to talk about, isn't it?'

'What's it got to do with you? It's my body. I can do what I like to it.'

'It is our business because we don't want you to die.'

I heard what he was saying, but I still didn't get it. I still thought it was up to me what I did to myself.

'You have asthma too, don't you?' he continued.

I nodded.

'Fancy stabbing yourself in the lung if you have asthma,' he joked. 'That was a bit silly, wasn't it?'

I couldn't really argue with that. The nastier I was with him the pleasanter he became, so I gave up after a bit. In time I came to realize that the doctors were all able to be charming and relaxed with us because it was the nurses who had to act as their enforcers. He told me I was going to be on suicide watch, which meant one of the nurses had to follow me absolutely everywhere I went, including the toilet. Every time I left a room he was right behind me, never taking his eyes off me. It was really winding me up and making me angry and unco-operative.

Although I wasn't much of a smoker myself, I realized that the other patients were congregating in the smoking room, so I spent most of my time in there, trying to stave off the boredom of having absolutely nothing to do for most of the day. I don't know what I was expecting the other patients to be like, but I was surprised by what a cross section they were. There were quite a few anorexics, both boys and girls, and there were some elderly people as well. There was one girl, Rebecca, who had the most incredible mood swings I have ever seen. One moment she would be totally silent and withdrawn, and the next she would be bouncing about all over the place like a kangaroo, literally jumping up and down and racing round the room. There was a little old lady called Eileen, who always had a white handbag clutched to her and was convinced that the Germans were invading.

'The Germans are coming, the Germans are coming. We must prepare ourselves. We need to get ready.'

There was an old guy called Fred, who was always puffing on a cigarette and had virtually no short-term memory at all. As well as smoking them himself, he would give cigarettes to anyone who asked and then when he ran out he would swear to the nurses that he had been robbed. Holly was a timid little teenage self-harmer who was too scared to even make eye contact. All she ever said was 'I'm sorry', which, sweet as she was, didn't half get on your nerves after a few hours. God knows what had been done to her in the past to make her so anxious to apologize all the time.

'They're all fucking nuts in here,' I said to Rebecca.

'We're all depressed, man,' she said. 'What are you in here for?'

'I accidentally stabbed myself,' I muttered, hoping that if I said it quickly enough no one would question it.

'Well, you shouldn't be in here then,' she said, looking truly concerned.

'How can you accidentally stab yourself?' Fred interrupted, but I ignored him.

'Where did you stab yourself?' Rebecca asked.

'In the chest.'

'What a load of bollocks!' Fred snorted contemptuously. 'He's a psychopath! He stabbed himself!'

Just as in prison, boredom was the greatest enemy. There were a few arts and crafts classes, but they couldn't keep that up all day. There was a pool table, but someone had wrecked it, so all we could do was sit around and talk and get on one another's nerves. I went back to my poetry writing again and someone came in to help me with that. There were supposed to be sessions with the psychiatrist too, but I didn't want to go over everything in my horrible past again, so I refused to go. They must have decided that my reluctance to talk showed I wasn't getting better, so they increased me to a 'section three', which meant they could keep me for up to six months, whether I liked it or not. I can't pretend that it was as bad as being in Lewes prison, but it made me feel pretty much the same. They must have thought they would wear me down, but I knew I had endured far worse than this and survived. They kept asking me who my family were and whether there was anyone I would like them to call for me.

'There's no one,' I kept telling them. 'I ain't got no one.'

I suppose they could have traced my family, since they had my name and birth certificate, but maybe I wasn't registered properly anywhere because Mum had kept me out of the system, imprisoned in the cellar for so long. The school my brother and sister went to only found out about me when one of them said something about having another brother who couldn't speak and never left the house. Until that moment I had been completely invisible to the outside world. It seemed that now I was so again. Maybe the hospital people did find Mum and she told them she didn't want anything to do with me. She was more than capable of saying that. If they did manage to trace any of my past life, they never said anything to me about it. It was as if I had none. I think there is a law about keeping psychiatric records separate from medical records too, so maybe that was the reason. If I had been forced to go back to Mum, it would have been far worse than anything else I had had to endure since leaving.

The doctor tried prescribing me drugs for my depression, which I resisted at first, as I didn't want to be sedated, but they weren't having it.

'If you don't take it voluntarily, we'll have to force you,' the nurses warned. I had seen enough of their tactics on other patients to know they meant it, but I still wasn't willing to just roll over and do what they told me without a fight.

The first one they gave me was an antipsychotic drug called Chlorpromazine. The moment they said what it was when they brought me the tablets, Fred started shouting at me not to take it because they were just trying to put me to sleep, so I flicked the tablet out of the nurse's hand. Next thing I knew the nurse had me down and was restraining me, pushing my head on the floor while his colleague hit an alarm button, which brought four or five others running in, all of them huge and none of them willing to take any notice of my shouts for mercy. They dragged me to the dormitory, pinned me to my bed and injected the drug into my arse without saying another word. It felt as if they were punishing me for refusing to talk to the doctor.

'What's all this aggression for?' I wanted to know when they finally relaxed.

'You wouldn't take your medication,' one of them said, avoiding making any eye contact.

Fred had been completely right. The Chlorpromazine was basically a tranquillizer and muscle relaxant that turned me into a zombie. Even a small dose would have dried out my mouth and tongue and made me feel dizzy and nauseous. The dose they actually shot into me on the bed must have been enormous, because it basically put me to sleep for two days; even on the third day I could barely move and it was as if everything going on around me was in slow motion.

For a while I had to admit they had got me beaten, and I started taking the tablets they gave me because I knew the alternative of being pinned down and injected would be worse. But it wasn't the last time they found cause to wrestle me to the floor and whenever they did it they were even rougher than the coppers had been on the night they arrested me with Jake on the night that my baby had been born.

Even after that incident I just didn't seem to be able to stop myself from answering back and making a nuisance of myself. I would try to keep a lid on it but it's hard to repress your real personality twenty-four hours a day, seven days a week for months on end. I got the distinct impression that some of the nurses enjoyed it when a patient played up a bit and they were able to indulge in a bit of aggression. Maybe they were as bored in that place as we were.

Eventually the doctor must have decided they had broken my spirit of rebellion and that it would be safe to take me off suicide watch and to stop telling the nurses to follow me around everywhere. This was a relief for me and a mistake for them. Despite the drugs and despite the fact that I didn't talk about it to anyone, the shadow of depression was still looming over me, threatening to swallow me at any moment. I still wanted to get free and if I couldn't physically escape from the building, then I was going to take the other option and kill myself if I could find any way of doing it. It seemed to me as if the doctors were never going to let me go any other way.

I had noticed that unlike me and the other more difficult patients, Rebecca was allowed to have a cord on her dressing gown because she wasn't considered to be a high risk. I watched her like a hawk for a few days and the moment she left the gown on her bed when no one else was around I slid the cord out of its loops, went to the toilet and hid it above a loose tile in the ceiling.

When the nurses realized the cord was missing they all went mad searching for it, stripping down all our bunks and emptying out our bags and lockers, but none of them suspected me or thought to look in the toilet ceiling for it. I was in no hurry to use it, knowing that an opportunity would arise again sooner or later, just as the opportunity of taking the cord had in the first place. Just knowing it was there, waiting for me, was a comfort. I waited a week, by which time the staff seemed to have given up searching and forgotten about it.

Deciding that the time was right, I made my way into the toilet as casually as I could, having ensured there was no one else around. I went into the cubicle and locked the door. Standing on the rim of the bowl, I lifted the tile and took down the cord, tying one end to a sturdy metal pipe that ran all the way along the top of the cubicles. I knotted a makeshift noose around my neck with the other end.

I knew that it wouldn't be long before one of the nurses came in for a routine check, so I had to work fast. As soon as the knots were tight, I stepped off the toilet to kill myself. The knots held and the pipe took my weight, leaving me with my feet swinging a couple of inches off the floor. I felt a crunching sensation in my neck and I was immediately gasping for breath as my natural survival instincts struggled to take over. I still wanted to die, but the pain was frightening me. I didn't think I could go through with it: it was going to be too painful a way to do it. Even as I struggled for breath, I told myself that if I just stuck it out for a couple of minutes the pain would all be over and I would never have to worry about anything ever again, but still my brain wouldn't obey me and stop fighting to survive.

It felt as if my face was exploding and I could hear voices in the distance. The nurses must have been able to hear something going on, because they kicked the door in just as I passed into unconsciousness.

When I woke up I was back in a bed in the Accident and Emergency ward of the hospital, with my neck and head braced in a stiff collar and my hands tied once again to the bars at the side. The pain was terrible. They had an oxygen mask over my face, but I was still gasping for air and there were drips going into my arm again. The psychiatric nurse who had been the main one following me around during my first few weeks was standing guard beside the bed.

'You've got us into so much trouble, you have,' he said when he saw my eyes had opened. At least that was some consolation, as if I had managed to get one over on them despite all their efforts to keep me pacified and under control.

When I finally got to see a mirror, I was shocked by the amount of damage I had done to myself in such a short time. My face and neck were a picture; with virtually every blood vessel having burst, my eyeballs were vivid red. They told me I had snapped a collarbone too and damaged my brain in some way by starving it of oxygen. I had in short made a complete mess of the whole thing and now I wanted to be dead even more than before.

I had to stay in the neck brace for weeks as the doctors waited for everything to settle back down, with a nurse guarding me twenty-four hours a day. The only good thing to come out of the whole episode was that they weren't able to force the tranquillizers down me any more because of all the other medication I was now taking. The nurses were actually quite nice to me now, and even untied my hands after the first week. Unable to swallow anything, I had to survive on liquids. They tried to get me to let them push a tube down my throat, but I wasn't having that and they didn't insist.

When I was finally taken back to the unit six weeks later, I found that the doctor had gone, apparently forced to resign because of what I had managed to do on his watch. I knew as I walked through those doors, with a nurse close on my heels, that they were never going to let me out now, and they were going to be watching me every second of every day. I was convinced that if I didn't take matters into my own hands I was going to be in there for the rest of my life. I had to find a way to escape.

Now they diagnosed me as being schizophrenic, with two distinct personalities: one silent, aggressive and sullen, the other loud, excitable and hyperactive. They thought they needed to calm down the hyper side, but it was the other personality that really worried them because they thought it was that one that made me want to kill myself.

Nothing much had changed while I was away and the same patients were all hanging around in the smoking room when I walked back in. They gave me a nice welcome home, the girls running over and hugging me.

'I'm so sorry,' Holly wailed, as always.

'You got me into a load of shit by using my dressing-gown cord,' Rebecca complained.

'They've confiscated bloody everything because of you,' Fred grumbled, puffing on an inevitable cigarette. 'Pencils, rubbers, everything. Bloody fool.'

I felt bad about being the cause of their lives becoming even worse than they were before and I decided to keep a low profile for a while. I was very docile with the staff, taking whatever tablets they gave me without complaint. My collarbone was still weak and I knew that if they felt they had cause to restrain me they might very well snap it, and I didn't want to go through all that pain again.

The new doctor decided to put me in for electric shock treatment, which was supposed to stimulate the brain or something. It was the most horrible experience imaginable, leaving me feeling as if my head had exploded. I had it four times but it gave me migraines and they had to stop. With every new indignity that they forced on me I became more determined to find a way to get out.

Six months after I got there, workmen were doing some work on the ventilation system, including in the toilets. Because I was now walking around like a zombie, the staff were beginning to loosen up on the security and not following me every moment. On a visit to the bathroom, in the cubicle where I had tried to hang myself, I noticed they were fitting a big vent into a hole in the wall and that the workmen had only temporarily covered it with a sheet of plastic. They had attached a grill to the outside wall, but it didn't look too sturdy and I thought there might be a chance I could kick my way through it. I saw an opportunity to hatch a plan and went away to think about it.

I couldn't risk trying to go at that moment, because my bag was still upstairs in the dormitory and there were a lot of staff around who would notice if I went to get it and then carried it into the toilet with me. There was a part of me that wanted to make a dash for it there and then, but I couldn't bear the thought of losing the few possessions I had, like my clothes and Dad's watch. I still used to wear Dad's watch sometimes, even though it didn't work any more, but that day it was in the bag.

'Why do you wear a watch that doesn't work?' people would ask.

'It was my dad's,' I'd say, 'and he's dead.'

That always shut them up.

I knew that there was a moment each evening when the nursing staff changed over shifts and for a few minutes there were always fewer male staff on the ward. If I was going to try anything, that would be the best moment to do it. I knew I had to make my move that week, before the workmen came back and finished the job off, filling in the hole.

The next evening I brought my bag down with me to the community room, trying to look casual.

'What are you carrying your bag around for?' one of the nurses asked.

'People keep smooching in it, so I'm keeping it with me,' I said.

'Do you know who it is?'

'I don't, no.' The lies kept flowing now I'd started. 'It was lying open and I'm really fussy about who touches my stuff.'

He seemed to accept this explanation, and the next day, when I did the same thing, no one said anything.

I needed an accomplice to cause a distraction at the moment of escape and make a noise to cover the sound of me kicking my way through the grill, so I asked Rebecca, knowing that she would do anything for a laugh.

'I need to get out of here, Becky,' I whispered. 'Please help me.'

'Right,' she said, rubbing her hands together gleefully. 'Which nurse shall I go for? We could each choose one to dive on.'

'I don't think that's going to work,' I said.

I told her the exact moment I wanted her to hit the alarm button upstairs, having counted the number of seconds it would take me to walk from the community room to the toilet. It wasn't that easy getting the concept of counting seconds over to her, but I still thought she was the most likely of all of them to pull it off for me.

'When they ask you what happened afterwards,' I said, 'just say you fell against the button.'

I needed her to wait exactly a minute from the moment I said 'go' to give me the time I needed. I reckoned that by the time the staff had all run upstairs, realized there was nothing going on and come back down, I would be through the vent and away. Becky wasn't brilliant at counting, especially when she was on medication, so I couldn't be completely confident things would happen exactly when I needed them to. I showed her how to watch the second hand on her watch and wait for it to go all the way round.

The moment arrived and we both headed off, with Becky staring intently at her watch as she mounted the stairs. I got into the cubicle, with my bag over my shoulder, and closed the door. Sixty seconds had passed but everything was still silent outside, so I couldn't start. I had taken the plastic cover off the vent and I could feel the fresh air from the outside world on my face as I bent down and peered through to the grill. I had worked out that if I found I couldn't kick the grill out quickly I would just walk back to the community room and no one would be any the wiser.

Becky must have taken her eyes off her watch and missed the moment because it was at least three minutes before the bells started to go off and I kept expecting to hear a nurse coming in to see what I was up to in there. The moment they went off the ringing was deafening and I could spring into action without having to worry about making a noise. I could hear running feet on the stairs and shouting as I wriggled my way into the vent, feet first, and kicked hard at the grill. It was a tight squeeze, but I just fitted because I was so skinny. The grill was resisting my blows, although it felt as if there was some movement to it. One of the corners seemed to be coming loose and I remembered how when we were smashing the shop windows we had always concentrated on the weakest points. I channelled all my efforts on that one spot and it began to go, eventually springing away from the wall. One more kick and suddenly it flew away, landing with a clatter outside.

I wasn't sure what I would do next, but at least I was on the outside and I could work out how to get over the fence while the staff were all still trying to sort out what had happened with Becky upstairs. It wasn't until I emerged from the wall on the other side that I realized it backed directly on to the street. I didn't have to worry about getting through the grounds and over the fences: I was already free.

One or two passers-by gave me funny looks and I just smiled and nodded as if it was the most normal thing in the world for a man to appear feet first through a wall and drop into a street. Some of them must have realized that the building was a psychiatric unit, but they didn't seem to know what to do. Perhaps they thought I was dangerous and didn't want to tackle me. Maybe they just didn't want to get involved in someone else's business.

My heart was thumping, as I expected to hear shouting and running feet behind me.

'All right?' I said cheerfully to a couple of people who were staring with open mouths. 'I've been working in there and got locked in.'

I could see they didn't believe me, but they didn't say anything and I set off at a brisk pace, diving in and out of back streets to cover my trail as quickly as possible. Emerging from one ally into a main street, I saw a bus drawing up and the doors opening. It said it was going back to Plymouth. I jumped straight on, even though I didn't have any money.

'They've stolen my money,' I wailed to the driver. 'I don't know what to do.'

'Don't worry, lad,' he said kindly. 'Just take a seat.'

The doors hissed shut and as the bus pulled forward I felt a huge wave of relief come over me. I'd made it. I was free again, even though I had no idea what I was going to do next or where I was going to go.

Chapter Twenty-Four

On the Run

I arrived back in Plymouth with my trusty bag still over my shoulder, six months after leaving on the train to Cornwall. I didn't want to go back to Lulu's flat because she would ask all sorts of questions, and I felt a bit guilty about just walking out on her without saying anything and then not getting in contact for such a long time, so I sauntered back to Colin's flat as if nothing had happened.

'Where the fuck have you been?' he asked when he saw me walk in. He looked genuinely pleased to see me, which was a nice feeling.

'I've been in a mental hospital,' I said casually. 'They said I was a schizo. I only just escaped.'

'You're not a nutter,' he said. 'How did you get out?'

He was laughing so hard as I told him the whole story that he set me off too. It felt so great to be back amongst friends that I quite forgot that it was living with Colin that had nearly driven me mad in the first place.

'I probably need to move out of the area,' I said later that evening, when we were mellowing out, 'because they're bound to be looking for me, since they think I'm a high-risk patient. If a copper stops me for anything around here, I'm going to end up being dragged back to the nuthouse so they can continue my "treatment". Have you still got the Granada?'

'Yeah, of course. Where do you want to go?'

'I don't know. Anywhere really. You got any ideas?'

'I know a few people in Watford. There's a lot of homeless people up there. We'd be OK there.'

'That'll do.'

So we packed a few possessions into our bags, got in the car and drove to Watford, which was a couple of hundred miles away on the north side of London. It took us hours, which made me feel safer with every mile that we travelled away from Cornwall.

There was a YMCA in Watford that Colin knew all about, where homeless people could get really nice rooms and meals without too many questions being asked. I had to give my name and details and I worried that they might lead the authorities back to other things, but it was a risk I was going to have to take if I didn't want to sleep on the street. Not only did I have a record for escaping from the psychiatric unit, and for skipping bail to go to Cornwall: I also still owed the money that I had been fined for the smash and grabs, since I hadn't been in a position yet to pay any of it back. I took the gamble that as long as I didn't get into any more trouble no one would bother to do a police check on me.

We stayed at the Watford YMCA for nearly a year in the end without anyone asking us any questions, by which time I was twenty years old. Colin and I stuck together the whole time, which inevitably led to me going back to drinking and smoking pot to pass the time and to dull some of the pain of depression now that I was no longer living on a cushion of tranquillizers. Although I needed the drink and drugs just to get me through the days, I felt guilty and inadequate for being unable to resist them. The guiltier I felt the more depressed I became and the more I wanted to escape through drink and drugs. It was a vicious circle. I would really have liked to have been able to fight my inner demons without those crutches, but I wasn't. Instead of addressing my problems, I was trying to run away from them, hide from them, drown them.

Our need for drink was soon out of control. It was leading us to stealing it when we didn't have the money to buy it and our cravings were driving us to take stupid risks. Mostly we would pinch it from the big supermarkets. We must have looked very suspicious, because at one of them I noticed the security man was watching every move we made from the moment we walked in. I sent Colin off to distract him while I grabbed a couple of bottles of vodka off the shelf and slipped them into the pockets of my coat. As I ran out the doors, I was grabbed by a man in a white coat who had been working on the cheese counter and had spotted what I was up to. Desperate to get away, I wriggled and struggled but he was strong and wasn't about to let go.

One of the bottles wobbled out of my pocket and burst on the pavement as I caught the second one just in time. Lashing out to try to get free, I accidentally whacked him on the head with the remaining bottle. He still didn't loosen his grip and I didn't manage to get away, which meant I ended up back in the police station yet again, charged with theft and with grievous bodily harm of the cheese man. I put my hand up to stealing the bottles but I really hadn't meant to hit the guy. In the end they dropped the charge to 'actual bodily harm' instead of 'grievous'. I really had learned how much easier it was when I cooperated with the police rather than giving them a load of cheek as I would have done a couple of years before. However, though I gave them my right name, I added a few extra middle names to muddy the waters a bit, and I still changed my date of birth to make it a bit harder for them to track down my records, since I assumed I was still listed as a missing person and I really didn't want to be carted back to the psychiatric unit.

I always found Colin very easy to be with, because he had been through many of the same experiences as me.

He'd been sexually abused as a child and there wasn't anything that we couldn't talk to each other about. Neither of us had any contact with our families and we both relied on one another for all our moral support. We actually became 'blood brothers' during one intense conversation, each cutting our wrists and pressing them together so that our blood mingled, bonding us for ever like some sort of baby Mafiosi.

As I still hadn't had any luck with meeting a girl, I was more than ever convinced that I was too ugly for anyone to ever love me. But one afternoon as I was waiting for a bus to pass so that I could cross the road I looked up as it drew level with me and made eye contact with a pretty girl who was sitting in a window seat. She held my gaze and broke into an instant smile, which made my heart skip. I wanted to get on the bus and talk to her, but the traffic was moving too fast and I was left standing by the road staring gormlessly, watching it disappearing. It's funny how the tiniest moments can sometimes touch something deep inside you, remaining as vivid memories long after other, bigger events have faded. For a long time I thought about that girl on the bus several times a day, imagining how I might be able to meet her and how we would fall in love and live happily ever after. It was what I wanted more than anything else in the world, but all I actually had was Colin and a fair amount of beer, vodka and pot.

I knew it was only a matter of time before the Watford police cross-referenced the fingerprints I'd given at the station and matched them up with the records in the other cities, so I told Colin it was time we moved on again. He was a bit reluctant, because he liked life in Watford, but in the end he realized that there was no choice and gave in. We climbed back into the faithful old Granada and headed north to Bradford in Yorkshire, with him moaning all the way.

Although he was a good mate, I didn't trust him any more than I trusted anyone else. I was pretty sure that once we got there he would wait till I wasn't watching and then take the car and drive back down south. Remembering how Jake's betrayal had led to virtually everything that had gone wrong in my life since then, I was determined to get in first. If there was one thing I had learned, it was not to trust other people, especially other alcoholics.

When we arrived in Bradford, he hopped out to buy us something to eat, leaving me waiting in the car. The moment he disappeared into the shop I slid across behind the wheel and drove off. I bought myself a load a beer and tried to drown out the feelings of loneliness and vulnerability that threatened to overwhelm me now that I was sitting alone in a car in a strange city watching the light fade. Without Colin there to distract me I thought about everything that had gone wrong and remembered just how shit my life was. Not only did I not have a girl-friend, but I didn't even have a friend who I felt I could trust. I was pretty sure that sooner or later the police would catch up with me, and they would either put me back in prison for clocking the cheese man or stick me back into a nut house. Neither of these options seemed bearable at that moment.

It all seemed so hopeless and taking another slug of beer was my only hope of making it feel better, and then another and another. Alcohol has a habit of taking all your normal thoughts and twisting and exaggerating them even further, convincing you to do things that you would never do if you were sober. I wanted to die in order to end all the pain, but I didn't want to stab or hang myself, because I already knew how much both of those methods hurt. Since I had the car, I decided to use it to gas myself. If I was drunk and falling asleep, I reasoned, I wouldn't feel a thing.

I had to find a way of piping the fumes from the exhaust into the car, so I drove myself to a nearby DIY store and bought everything I needed. Next I drove to a deserted industrial area where I was sure no one would ever find me. I fitted one end of the hose to the exhaust pipe and pushed the other end through the back window, taping up the gap to make sure all the fumes stayed inside. Then I set about getting really drunk. As I felt myself drifting towards unconsciousness, I switched the ignition back on and drifted off to sleep.

I have no idea what happened after that, but something must have made the engine cut out because the next thing I knew I was waking up in the car, surrounded by police. Maybe I had bent the pipe too sharply and the fumes had gone back in and cut the engine. As they dragged me out of the car, I realized it was morning. The rest of the world had woken up and come to work, and someone had spotted me in the car with the pipe going into the window.

By the time they got me to the hospital they knew everything about my past and they had me in a decompression chamber to get my lungs clear of anything I might have breathed in before the engine cut out. They locked me into it with latches with my arms pinned to my side, and the pressure on my ears was horrible, as if I was coming down too fast in an aeroplane, making me shout at them to stop and let me out, kicking and punching the sides.

'You'll be out in a minute,' someone said.

They didn't tie my hands when they took me back to the wards, which I thought was decent of them, but the coppers were hanging around to make sure I didn't try to do another runner. Another psychiatrist came to see me, reminding me of everything I had been through already, and I was sectioned for another twenty-eight days so that they could have another go at working out what was wrong with me.

'Listen,' I said, 'if you think you are going to be knocking me to the floor and sticking needles in my bum and zapping electricity through my head, you can think again.'

'No,' he said. 'There won't be anything like that. It's not a secure unit where we're sending you. It's a nice place.'

I doubted that very much, but I have to say, if you are going to go into psychiatric care, Bradford is the place to do it. Compared to the previous unit it was brilliant. The staff were really nice and helpful, and I had a lady doctor who never pushed me. Initially they talked about sending me back, but she vetoed that idea.

'As you are of no fixed abode either here or there,' she said, 'we might as well just keep you here. What would be the point of spending NHS money to send you half way across the country?'

Because they had decided I was mentally ill, the police couldn't do anything about the other charges, which I couldn't resist teasing them about.

'You can't do anything to me,' I grinned, 'because I'm mentally ill.'

'We'll wait,' one of them said, 'and get you when you come out.'

To be fair they had been very reasonable with me. One of the sergeants had sat with me for a bit.

'Nothing's worth killing yourself for,' he said. 'You're young, you can do anything you want. Why would you want to end it all? Just get yourself better, face up to whatever it is you've done, take a slap on the wrists and then do something with your life.'

I was very short of money and wanted to sign on for my benefit payments, so I walked out of the unit the next day to sign on. Even though the unit wasn't meant to be secure, the staff reported me, knowing exactly where I was because I had to give my address as the hospital to the benefit officers and they immediately called them. One of the policemen who turned up was the same sergeant as before, but he didn't seem too bothered.

'What are you doing causing trouble in here, Joe?' he asked.

'I just want my money!'

'Come on, let's take you back.'

'Do you want me to cuff him, sarge?' his colleague asked.

'No, he's a good lad. He won't give us any trouble.'

He was right, because I never did give trouble to people who treated me right. I went back to the hospital with them and instead of telling me off as I expected the lady doctor gave me a cuddle. She seemed to instinctively know that however much I might be strutting around, inside I was feeling vulnerable.

'If you want to go out, Joe,' she said, 'why don't you do it properly with one of the nurses? If you just walk out without telling anyone it's going to get you into trouble, isn't it?'

'Yeah,' I said, good as gold. 'Fair enough.'

Any minute I expected someone to throw me to the floor and ram a needle up my arse, but they never did. They didn't insist I took any drugs apart from a few sleeping pills to ease my worries while I went cold turkey yet again to get off the drink, and no electrical treatments. They nursed me with a gentleness I hadn't experienced before and suggested that I did some talking. It was to be the first proper psychotherapy I had really had.

'I'm not letting you out of here until you are ready,' the doctor told me, but the way she said it made me feel protected rather than threatened as I had felt in the other place.

I spent a lot of time lying down, listening to soothing music and talking about the things that worried me. And that led on to anger management classes. I trusted her to keep my secrets and started to open up a bit more about the things that had been done to me as a child. I was encouraged by how shocked she was at the things I had suffered. I felt that finally I was being listened to and believed. They could have sectioned me for longer than the twenty-eight days, but they said they would rather I stayed voluntarily. I liked that idea and so I did what they wanted.

For some reason, after I had been there about six months, I got it into my head that I wanted a passport. I think it started because I wanted to have a form of identification so that I could do things like open a bank account. I had built up some money from my benefits once they started giving them to me and I wanted to look after it properly, like everyone else, instead of sticking it under my mattress. The staff wanted me to as well, because they were worried it would go missing and everyone would fall under suspicion. The doctor helped me with the application form and the passport was sent to the hospital.

As I sat looking at my picture in this official document, I felt the familiar urge to move on. It was nice in the hospital and the people had been incredibly kind to me, but I didn't want to stay there for the rest of my life. I thought I was strong enough now to stay off the drink and be a good boy, but I didn't want to face the police, so I decided to disappear again while no one was looking. I managed to get hold of a screwdriver and unscrewed one of the windows one afternoon, chucked my bag through, squeezed through after it and made a run for it again.

Chapter Twenty-Five

A Bit of a Houdini

This time I made my way straight to the railway station, although I had no idea where I would take a train to. Pausing for a moment on the concourse to take in what was going on around me, I heard an announcement coming over the tannoy for a train which was about to leave. I was anxious to get moving as quickly as possible.

'Can I buy a ticket on the train?' I asked a man in uniform who was standing at the barrier.

'Yeah,' he said. 'Hop on.'

As I walked through the carriages to find a seat and the train began to move slowly away from the platform, I felt strangely elated at the thought of starting over again. My sessions with the psychotherapist had lifted my spirits and made me feel that I could cope with life on my own now, that I was ready to give it another try. I chose to ignore the fact that there would now be a missing persons report from the Bradford hospital as well as the previous one, and the police in Watford were still after me for the cheese man incident, not to mention the problems after I was caught for the smash and grabs, which had never been sorted out. I decided there was nothing I could do about any of that, so I might as well not think about it all.

As I strolled out of the station, wondering which direction to turn in order to start my new life, two British Transport policemen called me over, putting an abrupt end to my optimistic mood.

'There've been a spate of crimes committed on this station,' one of them said in quite a friendly manner. 'Do you mind if we search you?'

'I've just come from fucking Bradford,' I said, showing them my ticket. 'You can search me if you like. I've got nothing to hide.'

I handed my bag over to one of them while the other patted me down. I was willing myself to keep quiet and not antagonize them, but I was already feeling threatened and vulnerable and wanting to lash out.

'What's your name and date of birth?' the one patting me down enquired.

'What do you want that for?' I asked, sensing that I was being drawn back into their net.

'It's all right,' his colleague said. 'I've got his passport here.'

He opened it up to scrutinize it and then they radioed my details into their station. I felt a sickness of anxiety knotting my stomach but I forced myself to stay calm. Maybe they wouldn't make any of the connections immediately and they would let me go. Once I had disappeared into the streets, I would know to keep my passport better hidden. The radio crackled back into life, bringing the information that I was wanted by the Watford police. I had been free for only a few hours before I found myself sitting in the back of a police car again, being taken into custody while they did a bit more research into my background. It wasn't long before they discovered I had done runners from two different hospitals.

'Bit of a little Houdini, aren't we?' one of the officers joked as the information kept on coming through. I rather liked the idea that I could escape from anything. At least it meant I was good at something and it seemed to quite amuse the coppers. It was better than just being someone who robbed commuters at stations. I spent a few hours sitting in a cell while they tried to work out what everyone wanted to do with me.

'Apparently we're going to have to take you to a psychiatric unit here,' they told me eventually.

I shrugged, thinking I would just walk out again the moment their backs were turned.

'You won't be getting out of this one quite so easily,' they said, as if able to read my thoughts.

When we arrived later in the day, I could see what they meant. This was a secure unit and it was on the second floor of a tall building, so there wasn't going to be much chance of me making an escape through a window or a hole in the wall. Still feeling cocky from my previous successes at escaping, I tried walking out the front doors on the first day, but they were made of steel and firmly locked and guarded. There was no chance of getting out that way.

When they contacted the doctor in Bradford, she said she wanted me to go back there to continue with my therapy. I suppose she wanted to see the job through to the end, which was fair enough. The doctors were happy to do that because they wanted to save the money and get me off their patch. I wasn't averse to the idea myself, as this place seemed to me to be full of serious nutters, but I also knew that if they got me back to Bradford they would be watching me much more closely and I might not be able to get away again for a long time.

'We can't get you back there for a couple of days,' the doctor told me, 'because they haven't got a car to spare and they need to send a couple of nurses as well to make sure you get there.'

All I could think was that I wanted to get free again before I had a pair of big psychiatric nurses escorting me back to Bradford. I set about re-checking the whole of the unit for possible escape opportunities. None of the windows opened more than a couple of inches and it would have taken more than a screwdriver to get out of them. As I wandered around, trying to look casual, I saw the cleaning lady unlocking the door to her laundry store and disappearing inside, leaving the door ajar. I went over, pretending to be asking for something, and spotted a different sort of window on the other side of the room. It too was standing ajar, letting in a light breeze from outside, and it looked big enough for me to be able to get through. The cleaner was a lovely Jamaican lady and she didn't think anything was strange as I stood there chatting to her, eyeing up the window. There were piles of sheets and towels everywhere and I wondered if it would be possible to tie them together to make a rope I could climb down on, as I'd seen happening in movies sometimes.

On the second day I managed to slip into the room with my precious bag and hide while the cleaner was looking the other way. My heart was thumping so loudly I was sure she would be able to hear me as she bustled about before going out and locking the door behind her. I listened to her footsteps disappearing down the corridor before setting to work. I had a go at tying some sheets, but I wasn't sure that the knots were going to be strong enough to hold my weight. Although I was desperate to get out, I didn't fancy plunging two storeys down to the street below. I went over to the window and opened it wide, leaning out and looking around. I couldn't believe my eyes: there was a sturdy-looking steel waste pipe beside the window, running down the side of the building to the ground. I should be able to slide all the way down, like a fireman down a pole.

I clambered up on to the windowsill, forcing myself not to look down and concentrating on the pipe. With my bag over my shoulder, I gripped it hard and began the long climb down, sliding and bumping and trying to cling on, every muscle in my body screaming in protest. Once I had started, there was no going back, but as I got to the first floor I felt something slippery under my hands and realized the pipe had been greased with some black substance. I suppose it was to stop people climbing up and breaking in. Unable to keep any grip, I picked up speed at a terrifying rate, landing on the grass with a crash, my ankle buckling agonizingly under me.

The pain was terrible, but I could see a couple of hospital security men coming out of a door and running towards me from the other side of the building, and my urge not to be caught was stronger than my urge to avoid the pain. Since it was a secure unit, I knew from previous experience that they might really hurt me if they caught me. I ran and hopped, driven by a mixture of adrenaline and fear, and succeeded in getting away from them.

When I was finally able to stop and draw breath, I felt quite pleased to think I had managed to escape from a unit that everyone had said would be impossible to breach. Maybe I really was a modern-day Houdini. Since I had only just arrived in the town on the train a couple of days before, I had no idea where I was or what direction to head in. I just kept walking the streets and asking people where the station was until I eventually found it.

The first train was going to Gatwick and I wondered if I would be able to buy an air ticket to fly somewhere. I still had a couple of hundred pounds on me, which I had been planning to put in the bank, and I had my passport. I'd heard about how it was possible to pick up seasonal work in countries like France and Spain quite easily in order to earn enough to live.

Once I got to the airport, I went around the desks finding out how much the flights were and realized pretty quickly that £200 wasn't going to get me very far. Every way I looked I saw policemen with machine guns and bulletproof vests, and they all seemed to be looking directly at me, as if they knew everything about me and were just playing cat and mouse, biding their time before picking me up again.

'I just need to get to Spain or somewhere,' I told one of the women on the desks. 'Aren't there any cheap flights?'

'Have you thought of getting a ferry?' she suggested helpfully. 'They are much cheaper.'

Of course – why hadn't I thought of that?

'Where should I go for them?' I asked.

'Dover is probably your best bet,' she said.

I went back down to the train station and a few hours later I was sitting on a boat going across the English Channel to Calais. I couldn't believe that it could be this easy to escape from England when there were so many people after me. It felt brilliant to see the white cliffs disappearing behind me. It was as if I was wiping the slate clean and starting all over again. I was going to a new country with new people, who would know nothing about me and the great pile of records that had been following me from one secure unit to another. This was my chance to disappear from sight in England and start a new life.

Chapter Twenty-Six

Surviving Abroad

When I walked off the ship at Calais, I found the main road going out of town and settled down to hitch, hoping I would have better luck than I had had when I first left home. I was prepared for it to be hours before anyone picked me up, remembering how long I had sat beside the road before, but it didn't worry me. If the police came along, I had money and a passport and there was no reason for them to take me in. I had hardly been standing there any time at all before a car drew up and the driver offered me a lift. It was all going so smoothly I could hardly believe it. Maybe people are in a more open and generous frame of mind when they are coming out of a port like Calais.

Over the following few days I headed south and then west, across to Spain, really enjoying myself in the warmth, even though I couldn't speak a word of French or Spanish. The further south I travelled the easier it became to get lifts, as everyone seemed to become more relaxed and welcoming and willing to take a little time to help a young traveller on his own. I was living mainly on packs of digestive biscuits that I had stocked up on in Dover, and bottles of water, although some of the people who gave me lifts would buy me meals or share their sandwiches. I was amazed how open and friendly and helpful everyone was. I ended up in Gibraltar about ten days later. It was a place I had heard of, although I didn't know anything about it.

I had been sleeping rough all the way down, trying to make my money last as long as possible, but it was so warm at night it wasn't a problem. I was having such a good time I didn't want to stop. Having heard people talk about Italy, I decided I would like to go there next and see some of the sights I had heard other travellers describing. I hitched all the way back through Spain and France, along the Riviera and past Monte Carlo. It took a week to get there, mainly because some of my lifts would drop me off on little country roads and it would take me a while to find my way back to the main routes, holding up a bit of cardboard with 'Italy' written on it, but I wasn't in any great hurry. Sometimes I was even picked up by tractors and dropped just a few miles further down the road with no idea where I was or which direction I should be heading in.

Once I got to Italy, I hitched all the way down to the south. I had been trying to find jobs as I went, because my money was beginning to run low even though I was sleeping rough and mainly eating biscuits, but without any success. It seemed everyone had already hired as many people as they needed for the sort of casual jobs that I was after. Someone told me there was a lot of work to be had on the Greek island of Crete. I discovered that in order to get to Crete I needed to catch a ferry from Brindisi to Athens, and then another out to the island.

The day I arrived in Crete it seemed to be market day, so I just kept going from stall to stall, asking if anyone knew of any jobs going. Most people didn't speak English, of course, and I only had about three words of Greek by that stage, so it was starting to look like an impossible task. I was beginning to despair of ever finding anything.

'Are you looking for work?' an English voice asked.

I was shocked to find that the couple behind the next fruit stall were both English. They told me they had a fruit farm and needed some help. I accepted happily, remembering the good times I'd had on farms in England, and they took me back with them at the end of the day.

It was another happy phase of my life despite the hard work, with a room of my own and plenty of sunshine, food and friendly people. I think part of me assumed that in such a lovely, happy-go-lucky place I was bound to finally find the love of my life, but it still didn't happen, the language barrier making everything even more difficult than usual. I stayed for about six months and managed to save a bit of money before I found myself growing bored with the idyllic lifestyle. I was surprised to realize I was feeling lonely and a bit home-sick for England. Having been away for so long, I thought that maybe the police and the doctors would no longer be looking for me. My self-confidence had also grown while I was travelling around Europe. I wanted to have another go at making a life for myself in England and renew my search for an English girl who spoke the same language as me and wanted to share my life.

One of the locals I became friendly with on Crete was a man who ran a car hire business. He rented me a jeep, which I really liked driving around the little winding roads with the top down and the wind and sun on my face. I decided to use it to drive myself back to Italy and on home to England, rather than going back to living my life at the side of the road again. Despite everything that had happened to me over the previous few years, I still had a bit of Mum's influence in me, a belief that if I really needed something it was all right to just take it and face the consequences later, just as I had with the pig's head.

Getting to the mainland was no problem. On the ferry from Athens to Brindisi my spirits were high from being on the road once more and I got talking to a young American couple. I told them what my plans were, not really thinking that I was doing anything particularly wrong. They could immediately see that I shouldn't have taken the car off Crete without permission and told me off in no uncertain terms. I think they must then have grassed me up to the ship's captain, because as I drove off the ferry at Brindisi I was pulled over by the police, who dragged me out of the car and took me into custody. I couldn't understand a word they were saying and they kept punching me and pushing me around, hitting me with a baton during the interview process. I'd heard from other people that Italian prisons were a lot more violent than British ones and I started to feel really nervous that I might end up in a Brindisi version of Lewes, unable to speak the language and not understanding any of the rules or customs.

I was angry with myself for yet again messing things up when they had looked as if they were going well for me. Why could I never be satisfied when I found honest employment in nice places, as with Andy in Cornwall and with the couple on the fruit farm? Why did I always have to be searching for something more, something to fill the empty void in my heart? Was I never going to be able to break this cycle of behaviour, which kept pulling me back down? I could feel the familiar black cloud of depression rising inside my head, making me want to find a quick way to put an end to my own life.

To my relief the police decided in the end to put me back on the ferry to Athens so that I could face the music there. Because of my time in Crete I felt that I understood the Greeks better than the Italians, but I was still very frightened at the idea of ending up in a Greek prison.

The ship's captain came to see me as they brought me on board and seemed to be really sorry about what had happened.

'Why did you do this?' he asked, and I couldn't really come up with an explanation.

'Please don't take me back,' I pleaded after we had been chatting for a few minutes.

'I have to,' he said, spreading his hands in a gesture of helplessness. 'It is the law.'

'I bought a ticket,' I protested.

'But you took a vehicle,' he said, as if trying to explain it to a child.

'I rented it.'

'That had expired. You are not supposed to take it out of the country.'

Although he looked very regretful, the captain had to lock me into the cabin while he went off to prepare the ship to sail. I couldn't believe that I had got myself back into such a mess after things had been going so well for a year. Yet again I was imprisoned in a small room, my fate to be decided by other people, and I had brought it all on myself. My initial relief at getting free of the Italian police was now replaced by an increasing anxiety at what might lie ahead of me when we docked at Athens and they came to get me. The thought of having to deal with Greek police and prison, and maybe ending up being deported back to England and having to face all the charges that were waiting for me there, was more than I could bear. The depression was now boiling up and mixing with anger at myself and the whole world. In a fit of temper I smashed a mirror, picked up one of the jagged slices of glass from the floor and slashed wildly at my wrists.

By the time the captain had come back in to tell me that we were about to set off, there was blood all over the cabin. It was obvious they couldn't proceed with me in this state and he shouted orders for the ship to stay where it was. There were sailors running back and forth at his command. They had to get me off the ship again quickly so that it could sail with the other passengers.

Back on shore, an ambulance was called to take me to hospital in Brindisi while the ferry sailed off without me, so that my wrists could be stitched up, extremely roughly, before they chucked me back into a cell to wait for another sailing.

When the ferry was back the next day, the captain came to visit me and I could see that he felt bad about the way I was being treated. Maybe he also felt bad because he already knew that this time they were going to sedate me for the journey to make sure I didn't do the same again.

There was a doctor waiting for me on the ship this time who stuck a needle in me while the policemen held me down, so that I slept all the way across and didn't give them any trouble. When I came round, I found myself in front of the Athens police and the guy from the car hire company in Crete. Everyone was angry and shouting at me as I tried to wake up and clear my thoughts. It was like being trapped in a nightmare.

'You are facing a long time in prison,' a policeman threatened. 'And you need to pay this man for the damage to the car.'

They knew I had my earnings from the fruit farm on me, so they insisted that I paid it all over as compensation to the rental company. I think I would have owed him only about £100 for the time I'd actually had the car, but they made me empty my pockets, so in the end it cost me about four times that, which taught me a good lesson. They then kicked me out of the station with nothing – no money, no return ticket, nothing.

The only person I knew in the whole hot, busy city now was the captain of the ferry, so I went down to the docks to see if he would give me a free lift back to Italy, where I could hitch my way back to England. Wandering along the quay, having no real idea how to get on to the ship without a ticket, I heard my name being called.

'Joe! Joe!' I turned to see the first mate of the ferry running after me. 'How are you, Joe?'

'Can I go and see the captain?' I asked, still feeling groggy and confused from everything that had happened.

'Yes, of course,' he said, as if we were the oldest of friends. 'The captain feels bad for what happened to you.'

He put his arm round my shoulders and steered me on to the ship and along to the captain's cabin. The captain actually seemed pleased to see me, shaking me enthusiastically by the hand, sitting me down and getting me a cup of coffee. He seemed relieved that I hadn't been thrown into prison again.

'What will you do now, Joe?' he asked.

'I need to get back to England,' I replied, 'but they've taken all my money, so I don't know how to get across to Italy.'

'Don't worry,' he said. 'You stay in here. We'll be leaving for Brindisi again very soon.'

Not only did he give me a free trip back, but he also provided me with lunch and insisted on filling my bag with food and drink for the next stage of my journey. During lunch he even offered me a job on the ship, but I'd had enough of that ship by then and I didn't fancy the idea of spending the next few months going back and forth across the same stretch of water. He seemed disappointed by my refusal and gave me a huge bear hug when we docked.

I left the ship nervously, expecting the Italian police to jump on me at any moment and drag me off to the cells, or send me back to Greece again, saying I wasn't welcome in their country. But this time no one took any

269

notice of me as I walked away from the docks and went in search of the road that would lead me north.

Over the following days I hitched all the way up to France and then ended up back in Spain. Now that I was free of the police, I found that my urge to get back to England and risk being taken into custody again seemed to fade, although it wasn't replaced by anything else. I was a truly free spirit, drifting where life took me. What was there in England to go back for? I asked myself. And the answer was 'nothing'.

The food in my bag was running out by the time I got to Spain and since I had no money I knew I was going to have to find another job. I crossed the border into Gibraltar again, thinking it would be easier to find something in a country where English was widely spoken; it was hard work trying to make myself understood all the time in languages where I had no more than a few words. I went knocking on doors, asking if they had any jobs, and got one collecting glasses and wiping tables in a pub, which gave me a bit of money and a roof over my head. The landlord was a good bloke and I really enjoyed myself, feeling like part of a little community again. I worked hard and my boss was pleased with me.

One day, a few weeks after I arrived, there was a drunk in the pub who was bumping into everyone and spilling his beer all over the place. The other customers were getting really fed up and my boss asked me to do something about it because he was busy with something else. I was quite happy to handle the situation and walked over to the drunk.

'Can you leave, please?' I asked politely.

He wasn't shifting, so I put my hand on his shoulder and tried steering him gently towards the door. To my relief it worked and he moved, but as soon as we got outside he took a wild swing at me. That made me cross and I gave him a quick wallop, sending him to the ground, and someone called the police. It shouldn't have been a big deal, but what I hadn't realized was that the police in Gibraltar were part of the British force, so the moment they fed my details into their system my whole past record in England popped up. My heart sank.

I'd made friends with an ex-copper while I was at the pub and he came into the police station to see me.

'Please help me,' I pleaded, terrified of what would happen to me now. 'Please get them to let me go.'

'I can't do anything, mate,' he said. 'I wish I could. You're a wanted man.'

The landlord from the pub came in too, telling me how bad he felt that he hadn't dealt with the drunk himself. He tried to reason with the police on my behalf and hired me a solicitor, but it was too late by then: the authorities all wanted me back in England to answer all the various charges.

'There'll always be a job here for you if you want it,' he promised.

The police put me on the next plane to Gatwick and the British police met me as soon as I came out through customs. I had been away from England for a year by then. I was twenty-two years old.

Chapter Twenty-Seven

Boy Meets Girls

The officers at Gatwick were pretty friendly and they just took me to a cell to wait for some others from Watford to drive down and pick me up. It seemed I was finally going to have to face the music for the time I hit the cheese man with the vodka bottle.

'He's a good kid,' one of the Gatwick officers told them as I was handed over. 'He won't give you any trouble.'

They still handcuffed me to get me to the car, although they took the cuffs off once we were driving. They were very friendly all the way back, chatting about my situation and what I should do.

'Just explain everything to the magistrate,' one of them said. 'They won't be too hard on you because you're obviously a nice lad.'

It was kind of them to say so, but I didn't share their optimism, given my past experience.

By the time I was standing up in court, the authorities had uncovered the outstanding fines from the smash and grabs as well, which I still hadn't done anything about. They did notice, however, that I had done very well during the period when I was on probation in Cornwall, so they decided to give me another two years on probation, with a suspended sentence should I get into any trouble during those two years, and told me to pay £1,500 compensation to the cheese man, even though I didn't have a penny to my name. It was a big relief not to be going back to prison, but it still seemed like a major restriction after all the freedom I had experienced abroad. It also meant that under the terms of my probation I had to stay in Watford.

I had gone back to the YMCA building that I had stayed in before, so they bailed me to that address. One of the first people I bumped into there was Colin, who was still not happy with me for driving off and leaving him in Bradford about two years earlier.

'You bastard,' he said, the moment he saw me.

'You're a twat, you,' I said, thinking quickly on my feet. 'How long were you in that shop for? I was waiting and then coppers came along and booked me.'

'Oh.' He stopped shouting. 'I didn't know that, mate. What happened then?'

'They put me back in a mental hospital,' I said, reverting to the true story now that he had calmed down.

I really didn't want to stay in Watford because it felt like taking a step backwards when what I wanted was to make another fresh start. I'd been told that Hereford was nice and since I didn't know of anywhere else I asked the probation people if I could move there. They were a bit doubtful, since I had no one to go to, but they could see the sense of me making a new start away from Colin and the rest of them in Watford and arranged a hostel for me down there.

Yet again I was starting over in a strange town where I knew no one. Was this going to be the pattern for the rest of my life? Or was this going to be the place where I would finally meet the girl who would prove to be the love of my life?

After a few days I got myself a little ground-floor flat on Green Street, where the landlord was willing to accept people who were on social security. I got another job in a pub and started to make some friends around the area, including a guy called Patrick and a pretty, sun-tanned girl called Jenny who I dated a few times. Eager to court her properly, I would buy her bouquets of flowers every week from a sweet Welsh florist who had the loveliest lilting accent.

Jenny's dad was a retired SAS officer, which scared me a bit but also impressed me a lot. They were a really nice family and there were pictures all over the house of him with his fellow soldiers. I think it was because of Jenny's dad that I developed an interest in firearms and the army. I got an SAS tattoo and started collecting replica guns, just as a hobby, putting them up on the wall of my flat in their cases. Patrick used to love these guns and in order to wind him up I pretended they were real.

'How did you get them then?' he wanted to know.

'Oh, I know a few people in the arms business,' I said casually.

He was swallowing everything I told him, so I kept making up more and more stories just to see the look on his face. When it was announced that the Queen was due to come to Hereford to open something or other I developed my stories to a whole new level.

'I've got a contract to take her out,' I told Patrick, with a totally straight face.

The next thing I knew armed police officers were kicking my door in on the day before the Queen was due to arrive, telling me they had information that I was planning an assassination. I tried to explain that the guns were just replicas and that I was joking, but they weren't taking any risks. They kept me in custody until the royal visit was over and they took away the guns to test, which involved drilling holes in them. In the end they released me without charge, once Her Majesty was safely out of the town. They knew all about my record and informed my probation officer of the incident. My probation period had been just about to end but they extended it because of that, which struck me as ridiculous, although I could see that I had brought it on myself by winding

Patrick up without thinking what the consequences might be.

Jenny and I went out together for a good four months before she met someone else and dumped me. It was perfectly predictable because she deserved better than me, but I was still gutted. Every girl I ever liked ended up rejecting me when the one thing I wanted and needed more than anything else was to feel loved and secure. Convinced yet again that I was too ugly and bad for anyone to ever love me, I plunged back into the same dark places I had been to before and took an overdose, wanting yet again to escape from the pain.

As usual I messed it up and found myself waking up, still alive, in the hospital. Jenny's mum came to see me, which was a sweet gesture, but not enough to make me feel any better.

'You're young,' she said, guessing why I had done it, even though I didn't say anything. 'There will be plenty more fish in the sea.'

It doesn't matter what people tell you at moments like that: you still don't believe things will ever work out or that you will ever feel happy again. At the same time I did know she was right and I really didn't want to be going back into psychiatric units. I wanted to cope with this setback like a normal person, have a cry, pick myself up and get back in the race. I was supposed to be seeing a psychiatrist in the hospital but I decided not to do that. I knew that once they started asking questions I would

277

have to go over all the old stuff yet again and since I'd messed up killing myself yet again I just wanted to have another go at getting on with my life. I discharged myself, walking out of the hospital and going back to my little flat on my own.

Patrick knew what I was going through and was a good friend. He kept me cheerful and did stuff for me like teaching me how to drive properly by introducing me to his uncle, who was a driving instructor. Because of them I actually took a test and got a licence. I now had a passport and a driving licence, and with each of these little steps forward I was learning how to be a functioning member of society, being taught all the things that my mum and dad should have been able to help with if Dad hadn't died and Mum hadn't hated me with such a vengeance and wanted to do nothing but hurt me.

Another of my friends was designing and selling graphics and he gave me a job, teaching me how to work with computers. I found I had a bit of a talent for that and started to actually make some money at it. After a while I set up on my own, with the help of this friend, and became a full-time freelance graphic designer. I wasn't making loads of money, but I was earning enough to support myself, which was a good feeling.

That side of my life was all going well, but I still felt there was a hole at the centre of my existence because I still hadn't found anyone to love me or to share my life with. Having broken up with Jenny, I wanted to move on again, as I always had in the past, imagining that despite all my previous disappointments I would find what I was looking for in the next town I landed in.

I had finally worked out that whenever I turned to drink to escape from my depression I ended up in more trouble, so I fought really hard to stay off it. It had been drink that had fuelled me to go out smashing windows the night after I had held my baby, and it had also led to me hitting the cheese man and to stabbing myself and ending up in the psychiatric unit. Over and over again I had repeated the same pattern of behaviour and I knew that I couldn't afford to risk it any more. I had to learn to face life without the help of that deadly crutch.

As I drove home from work one night, another driver ran into the back of my car really hard, giving me a nasty case of whiplash, which led to me ending up in hospital again. Because of the injury I'd had before to my collarbone, I was in agony. This time, however, because I was all legal, I was paid a few thousand pounds' compensation, which gave me a little bit of money in the bank for the first time ever. I felt rich.

The girl with the pretty Welsh accent in the flower shop had made a big impression on me and I decided that I would like to go to Swansea next, where all the girls would sound like her. I had a little trailer for my graphics equipment, which was painted up with my logo and mobile number. I gave up the flat in Hereford, hitched the trailer to the car and headed off through

Monmouthshire, once more on the road in search of something or someone that would bring me happiness. I was close to twenty-three by then.

Although I had Swansea in my head because of the florist, I was still open to any other ideas that might crop up along the way, so when I saw a signpost to Barry Island I decided to take a little detour and find out more. There's something very romantic about the idea of any island, whether it's Crete or Barry, and even if it is attached to the Welsh mainland by a bridge.

Barry Island is a holiday destination with a beautiful beach, an amusement park, a promenade and all the other trappings of fun. It had a really nice relaxed feel to it, so I decided to stop there for a while and find a place to rent. Using some of my compensation money, I took a cheap, run-down flat on the promenade and settled in.

My graphics business fell to pieces a bit after that, but I wasn't too bothered. I had met a couple called Dean and Sharon, who were really good to me and introduced me to all their friends. Suddenly I was meeting girls and they seemed to be interested in me. Maybe I was finally maturing a bit and growing into my gangling frame, or maybe it was the holiday atmosphere of Barry Island, which loosened everyone up, but I actually found I was able to pull women successfully. I had a flash car and my own flat; I was made. I was able to push my depression to the back of my mind with a frantic whirl of sex and socializing. For a while it went to my head and I wasn't always as nice to the women I went out with as I should have been, using them in much the same way I had used drink in the past, as a distraction and a consolation. All my life I had been controlled and rejected by a variety of women, starting with Mum, and now that I'd broken the cycle I was enjoying my run of luck too much. And in the excitement I forgot that what I had been craving ever since I could remember was to find someone who would love me and who I could share my life with, not just a series of people I could sleep with and then send home.

One of the girls I really liked was mixed race and I was shocked by how many people seemed to have a problem with that. By that stage I had completely got past the racist feelings I had been left with by my childhood experiences and I found it hard to understand why I couldn't make other people see how wrong it was in the same way I had been shown when I first came down to London.

There was also a girl called Michelle who had recently separated from her partner. She was celebrating her twenty-first birthday in a place I used to go to called Al's Bar when I first noticed her and was struck by how pretty she was. I bought her a drink and she told me she had seen me around in a few clubs in Barry.

'I even bumped into you once or twice,' she said, 'on purpose. But you didn't notice.'

I was surprised by that, because she was strikingly beautiful. I certainly wasn't going to make the same mistake again. I wanted to take her back to the flat there and then, because all the other girls I had been seeing had been perfectly willing to do that, but she wasn't having any of it. She made it very clear that she was not 'that kind of girl', which I respected, just as I had when I met Lisa. Unlike Lisa, however, she stuck to her principles and wouldn't let me get anywhere over the next couple of weeks. I was becoming both frustrated and fascinated. This girl was very different to the others that I had been going out with recently. I also discovered that she already had two sons, a three-year-old and a one-year-old, who she was bringing up on her own. The more I found out about her the more I could see to admire.

When I met her I'd just booked myself a holiday in California, staying at a hotel across the road from Disneyland.

'Are you going to be coming back?' she asked when I told her about my plans.

'I don't know,' I said. 'I might just stay there. I'll see what happens.'

I did actually have a return flight booked, because you had to in order to be let into America, but I was planning to just wait and see what happened, taking each day as it came, as I had in Europe. I was also being devious and hoping that maybe Michelle would agree to give in and sleep with me if she thought it might convince me to come back. It worked and she came back to the flat with me on the night before my flight.

Chapter Twenty-Eight

California Dreaming

Arriving in California was like a dream come true. I could hardly believe that I was actually there, and being amongst the palm trees and sunshine I found it hard to imagine the darkness and misery of my early years. It was as if I had been reborn and was being given a chance to start my life afresh in an entirely different world.

The first week out there I went to Disneyland and did all the things I had been dreaming of doing for years, making up for some of the childhood I had missed out on. It was the best time of my life, and the more I did the hungrier I became for new experiences. Once I had exhausted the possibilities of Disneyland, I decided I wanted to see the real Los Angeles and hired a cab to take me to a nightclub in the city, armed with my passport so that they would know I was over twenty-one and allowed to drink, because I still looked a good few years younger than I was. I had to queue to get into the one I had heard about, but eventually I was admitted and had a fantastic night. The Californian women seemed so beautiful it was hard to believe they were real, which a lot of them weren't of course, this being the world capital of plastic surgery.

In the heat and noise and excitement of the club I met a guy called Jason and he invited me to join him at his table. He and his friends welcomed me as if I was their long-lost brother and I had a really good time, forgetting all about the outside world and my past and the demons that lurked in the back of my mind just waiting for an opportunity to re-emerge. I reckoned that if I partied long enough and hard enough maybe I could keep them at bay for ever.

In the early hours of the morning things began to slow down and Jason suggested we go back to his place. I accepted eagerly, never wanting the night to end, and when we got outside the club there was a huge limousine waiting for us. This was the first clue I had that Jason was seriously loaded. The next clue was his apartment, which was enormous and beautiful. It turned out that his dad headed up some big pharmaceutical company and gave Jason whatever he wanted.

I never went back to my hotel for the rest of my stay, apart from to pick up some clean clothes or my asthma medication, because Jason's whole family took me over and insisted that I stay with them, both at the apartment and at his father's house. They were as open and welcoming as Sue and her family had been, although their lifestyle couldn't have been more different. Kind, happy families were the greatest wonder in the world to me. I could hardly begin to imagine how different my life would have been if I had been born to different people.

It felt as if I was starring in my own personal movie and the idea of going back to Barry Island was beginning to lose its appeal. I confided to Jason that I never wanted to leave California and he asked his dad if they could find me a job and get me a work permit. His dad seemed to think it would be possible.

On one of my visits back to the hotel the receptionist told me that I had a phone message. It was from Michelle's mum, who I had never even met. Unable to imagine why she might be calling me, I rang the number she had left.

'Oh,' she said when I got through, 'so you're Joe.'

'Yes,' I said, cautiously, 'that's me.'

'Don't you think you had better come back to Wales?'

'Why?'

'Because you've got my daughter pregnant. She's throwing up and worried out of her mind and you're swanning around on holiday in Disneyland.'

Although I wasn't too thrilled by her tone, I could see why she might have been a bit fed up to find out her daughter was pregnant for the third time and looking as if she might still not have a man who would support her and help her bring up the child. I hung up and after taking a few minutes to digest the news I rang Michelle to ask her if it was true.

'Yeah,' she said. ''It's true.'

'Are you planning to keep it?'

'My mum doesn't believe in abortions.'

I was pretty sure that she felt the same way but wanted it to sound like it was her mother's decision, not hers, in case I tried to change her mind.

'I've just been offered a job out here,' I said, 'and someone is going to fix me up with a work visa.'

'You bastard,' she said and hung up.

I sat staring at the phone. How could this possibly be? After a life of rejection and never being wanted by anyone, I suddenly had to choose between two amazing options. On the one hand I was being offered a job and an apparently endless supply of beautiful girls in a land of sunshine and opportunity. On the other hand there was a really beautiful and lovely girl carrying my baby back in England, a girl who I thought the world of and who would come with a ready-made family for me to be part of.

As the shock wore off, I felt a knot of excitement growing in my chest. Michelle was going to have my baby! How brilliant was that? Although now I thought about it I couldn't be sure that Michelle would actually want me as a full-time partner; but even if she didn't I would still be able to see her all the time because of the baby, and I would be a dad, which was one of the things I had been longing for ever since my relationship with Lisa had collapsed. I remembered what it had felt like to hold my son in my hands and the memory made me feel almost sick with excitement at the thought of being able to do the same thing again. I could tell from the few words I'd just had with her mother that Michelle's family were unlikely to be approving of me as a suitable future son-in-law. I knew they were right too; Michelle was well out of my league, a really good, decent girl as well as a beautiful one. Why would she ever want to end up with someone as ugly and useless as me?

I picked the phone back up and redialled her number.

'I'll be on the next flight back,' I told her.

The moment I saw her again all thoughts of living in California vanished from my mind. I knew I wanted nothing more than to spend the rest of my life with Michelle and the kids, but I didn't dare to believe that she would agree to it because I knew the pain of another rejection would have been too much for me to bear. Doing some rough calculations in my head I reckoned I had about £3,000 left in my bank account, which I handed over to her as a gesture to show how determined I was to be a responsible father.

'I wish I could give you more,' I said, 'but that's all I've got until I can get my business going again.'

'So how are you going to live?' she asked, looking at the money a bit doubtfully.

'I'm not sure,' I admitted.

I felt a pang of sadness at the thought of having to give up my flat and go back to living in hostels or on the streets. I presumed I would have to sell my car too in order to raise a bit more money. I didn't want Michelle and the baby to have to go without anything if it was within my power to provide it.

'You'd better move in with me then,' she said, and when I looked across I could see she was grinning.

'Would you want me to?' I asked, unable to stop a similar grin from spreading across my face too.

'Of course I would,' she laughed. 'I love you, don't I?'

Epilogue

Michelle and I were married in March 1997. Kirsty-Lea was born a few weeks early, but she was still a healthy seven pounds. As well as living with Michelle and my two brilliant stepsons, Darren and Liam, who I was eventually able to adopt, I now had my own baby girl. In the coming years she was followed by Shannon and Paige. They are five very special and beautiful children.

Michelle and I trusted one another from the first day we got together. She has worked hard to keep me on the straight and narrow, out of trouble and out of hospitals. She has kept me off the drink and drugs and away from self-harming. There have been so many things that other people would count as normal but which I have had to learn from scratch. When any of the children told me they loved me, for instance, I found it hard to accept or to know how to respond.

How could any child love an adult? I couldn't even begin to understand that, maybe because I had loved Dad and he had been taken away from me. I also found it really difficult to accept simple kindnesses like birthday or Christmas presents, remembering all the teasing and bullying that my brothers put me through on my birthdays as a child. The fact that the kids would do something like that for me was too overwhelming for me to be able to cope with. I didn't mind celebrating their birthdays but I didn't want anyone drawing attention to mine because deep inside I remembered the pain that always led to.

Over the following years Michelle and I supported each other in everything we wanted to do. I had a lot of adjusting to do in order to be in a permanent relationship, which she helped me with patiently. Because of the way my mother had ruled my life for so long with such cruelty, I still found it hard to ever be told what to do by any woman, even someone I loved as much as Michelle, but we worked through that. I had anger management issues and at times it was hard for Michelle to cope with me.

Once she actually went to visit Mum without telling me, to try to understand better what had happened during my childhood. Mum didn't even try to deny anything, telling her that I'd deserved everything that had happened to me, that I had enjoyed the things that the paedophiles had done to me. Years later Michelle told me about the meeting and how she was physically sick after listening to Mum's vile boasting and very nearly went to the police station on her way back to the train. I had been afraid she was about to give up on me at that stage because of the way I was behaving, but I remember how she hugged me when she got home that day and promised that she would stay with me until we had worked through all my problems together, without telling me why. She was like a lioness protecting her cubs from the world.

Michelle's parents had never really made her go to school as a child, even though she was a bright girl. She was working as a nursing assistant while I stayed home to look after the kids, a role I really enjoyed, but she wanted to do more. As the children started to develop, Michelle decided she wanted to get herself an education. We both spent a lot of time discussing ways in which we could improve our lives and she decided to go back to college to do her A-levels and then started a psychology course at university, moving on to study speech and language therapy, partly because our daughter, Shannon, has had problems and we have had to learn new skills in order to help her. Now that Shannon is progressing better Michelle is moving on to midwifery. I am so proud of everything she has achieved.

I also went back to college once the kids were going to school, to study computers and expand on everything I had learned in Hereford. In 1999, using the computing skills I'd learned at college, I set up a website for the victims of child abuse, remembering how lost and alone I had felt both during the time of my abuse and afterwards when I set off into the world with virtually no life skills or self-awareness. If I could have had someone to go to through a website or by any other means, and could have felt free to talk about the things that I was afraid of and ashamed of, it would have changed my life radically.

I had told Michelle every detail of what had happened to me and she encouraged me in everything I wanted to do. Like other people I had told about my past, she also believed that my mother, my brothers, Amani and Uncle Douglas and all the men who came to Uncle Douglas's house should not be allowed to get away with what they had done to me and to the many other children like me that they used and hurt. Like many abused children, I initially wanted to sweep everything under the carpet and to try not to think about it. If you have been intimidated and beaten and brainwashed throughout your formative years, it is very hard to find the courage to turn round and stand up to the people you fear the most, even though you also hate them the most. She wanted to go to the police with everything I had told her, but that idea terrified me, for I was sure that Mum and the others would hunt me down if they thought I was grassing on them. I knew from experience what levels of violence they were capable of. Now that I had finally found a life full of security and love and well away from them, the thought of them arriving in Wales to look for me made me feel physically sick.

In the end I compromised and agreed that she could anonymously feed all the details through to *Crimestoppers*, the television programme. I heard from a distant cousin that Amani was arrested with a number of other men shortly after that, but I don't know if that was because of information we had provided or whether they were already after him.

I know I have come an amazingly long way from the terrible cellar where Mum kept me, and by using that experience to set up a website I feel some good has come out of it, but there is still so much to do and so many more children to be helped.

Mr Joe Peters
joe@crysilenttears.co.uk
www.crysilenttears.co.uk

Registered Charity No. 1069802
Mr Peter Saunders
Chief Executive
www.NAPAC.org.uk
Telephone Support Line **0800 085 3330**